The WAC Journal

Writing Across the Curriculum
Volume 24
Fall 2013

© 2013 Clemson University
Printed on acid-free paper in the USA
ISSN: 1544-4929

Editor

Roy Andrews

Managing Editor

Heather Christiansen, Clemson University

Associate Editors

David Blakesley, Clemson University
Michael LeMahieu, Clemson University

Editorial Board

Art Young, Clemson University
Neal Lerner, Northeastern University
Carol Rutz, Carleton College
Meg Petersen, Plymouth State University
Terry Myers Zawacki, George Mason Univ.

Review Board

Jacob S. Blumner, Univ of Michigan, Flint
Patricia Donahue, Lafayette College
John Eliason, Gonzaga University
Michael LeMahieu, Clemson University
Neal Lerner, Northeastern University
Meg Petersen, Plymouth State University
Mya Poe, Penn State University
Carol Rutz, Carleton College
Joanna Wolfe, University of Louisville
Terry Myers Zawacki, George Mason Univ.
David Zehr, Plymouth State University

Subscription Information

The WAC Journal
Parlor Press
3015 Brackenberry Drive
Anderson SC 29621
wacjournal@parlorpress.com
parlorpress.com/wacjournal
Rates: 1 year: $25; 3 years: $65; 5 years: $95.

Submissions

The editorial board of *The WAC Journal* seeks WAC-related articles from across the country. Our national review board welcomes inquiries, proposals, and 3,000 to 6,000 word articles on WAC-related topics, including the following: WAC Techniques and Applications; WAC Program Strategies; WAC and WID; WAC and Writing Centers; Interviews and Reviews. Proposals and articles outside these categories will also be considered. Any discipline-standard documentation style (MLA, APA, etc.) is acceptable, but please follow such guidelines carefully. Submissions are managed initially via Submittable (https://parlorpress.submittable.com/submit) and then via email. For general inquiries, contact Heather Christiansen, the managing editor, via email (wacjournal@parlorpress.com). The WAC Journal is an open-access, blind, peer-viewed journal published annually by Clemson University, Parlor Press, and the WAC Clearinghouse. It is available in print through Parlor Press and online in open-access format at the WAC Clearinghouse. *The WAC Journal* is peer-reviewed. It is published annually by Clemson University, Parlor Press, and the WAC Clearinghouse.

Subscriptions

The WAC Journal is published annually in print by Parlor Press and Clemson University. Digital copies of the journal are simultaneously published at The WAC Clearinghouse in PDF format for free download. Print subscriptions support the ongoing publication of the journal and make it possible to offer digital copies as open access. Subscription rates: One year: $25; Three years: $65; Five years: $95. You can subscribe to The WAC Journal and pay securely by credit card or PayPal at the Parlor Press website: http://www.parlorpress.com/wacjournal. Or you can send your name, email address, and mailing address along with a check (payable to Parlor Press) to Parlor Press, 3015 Brackenberry Drive, Anderson SC 29621. Email: sales@parlorpress.com

Reproduction of material from this publication, with acknowledgement of the source, is hereby authorized for educational use in non-profit organizations.

Contents

The WAC Journal
Volume 24, Fall 2013

ARTICLES

Evolutionary Metaphors for Understanding WAC/WID LAURA BRADY	7
Connecting WID and the Writing Center: Tools for Collaboration HEATHER M. ROBINSON AND JONATHAN HALL	29
WAC/WID Meets CXC/CID: A Dialog between Writing Studies and Communication Studies DENISE ANN VRCHOTA AND DAVID R. RUSSELL	49
Multidisciplinarity and the Tablet: A Study of Writing Practices JENNIFER AHERN-DODSON AND DENISE K. COMER	63
Committed to WAC: Christopher Thaiss INTERVIEWED BY CAROL RUTZ	83
Conversations in Process: An Observational Report on WAC in China MARTHA A. TOWNSEND AND TERRY MYERS ZAWACKI	95

REVIEW   111

Introducing Writing Across the Curriculum into China:
    Feasibility and Adaptation by Dan Wu
REVIEWED BY MYA POE

Contributors	117
Subscribing to and Publishing in *The WAC Journal*	121

Evolutionary Metaphors for Understanding WAC/WID

LAURA BRADY

IN THE RECENT AND IMPORTANT ESSAY, "A Taxonomy of Writing Across the Curriculum Programs: Evolving to Serve Broader Agendas," William Condon and Carol Rutz identify four types of programs: Foundational WAC, Established WAC, Integrated WAC, and WAC as Institutional Change Agent. These programs can be identified by key characteristics such as their primary goals, their funding, their structure or organization, and signs of their integration or success (362-63). To show how this valuable taxonomy works in practice, Condon and Rutz draw on concepts of location and momentum derived from quantum mechanics that they hope will "allow those within a program to gain a sense of place (of where they are, programmatically, in the universe of WAC programs) and a sense of movement (of what steps are available next, and of which might be desirable)" (360-61). When Condon and Rutz shift their taxonomy from static to dynamic description, they shift from a life sciences frame (biological taxonomies) to a physical sciences frame (quantum mechanics). There are distinct advantages, however, to be gained by extending the biology frame. Evolutionary metaphors for understanding WAC/WID complement rich description with dynamic causal analysis of a program's origins, adaptations, and threats; they allow us to consider location, movement, and other factors simultaneously.

This essay extends the evolutionary metaphor to two very different but very successful WAC programs (one at a small liberal arts college and one at a large public university) to show how we might develop and apply a heuristic that can help us explore the evolutionary potential of our WAC programs. That is, if Condon and Rutz's taxonomy helps programs situate and assess themselves in a national context and provides descriptive language that is easily understood by others *outside* of our field (379, 361), then an evolutionary metaphor can provide a useful means of internal study: a way of understanding the causes and conditions for a WAC program's origins and reproduction, mutations and adaptations, endangerment, or extinction.

Moving from taxonomy to evolutionary theory follows a historical pattern. Evolutionary theory represented the next scientific step beyond taxonomy for advancing our understanding of the natural world. Carl Linnaeus (Carl von Linné), author of *Systema Naturae*, 1735, is credited with establishing hierarchical structures for classifying organisms according to their physical traits and their methods of reproduction. His taxonomy relied on visible, observable characteristics. In the late eighteenth century, Cuvier's functional taxonomy superseded Linnaeus's descriptive taxonomy (Foucault 268). In contrast to the externally visible traits emphasized in Linnaeus's taxonomy, Cuvier was beginning to theorize internal causes and conditions that could account for differences and disruptions. "From Cuvier forward," Foucault argues, "it is life in its non-perceptible purely functional aspect that provides the basis for the exterior possibility of a classification" (268). Classification is still useful for Cuvier, but he shifts the categories from highly specific traits to very general principles. In his emphasis on function, Cuvier thus helps lay the ground for Charles Darwin's theory that species formation depends on the natural selection of traits that help an organism adapt to its environment *and* reproduce successfully.[1]

Darwin's theory of natural selection relies on environmental conditions, mutations, and change. His famous finches adapted to different environmental niches on the Galapagos, with the most relevant factor being the type of available food. In a different place, adaptive coloration may have led Darwin to study predatory/prey relationships. The point remains: if a particular mutation lines up with an environmental niche and gives an organism a reproductive advantage in terms of a food source, protective coloration, or something else it can productively exploit, that trait gets passed along to subsequent generations and eventually a new species is formed. WAC also speciates by adapting to its local environment. Evolutionary metaphors help explain and explore patterns, interrelationships, and the conditions under which a program can thrive. The metaphor can also help us understand that not all mutations are adaptive or successful, and that certain conditions threaten a program's survival.

Evolutionary and ecological metaphors are, of course, not new to WAC discussions or to more general discussions of writing practices. In 1986, Marilyn Cooper argued for "The Ecology of Writing," where writers are part of a varied and inherently dynamic system. Rather than paying attention to individual writers and their immediate contexts, Cooper asks us to attend to the ways in which, "all the characteristics of any individual writer or piece of writing both determine and are determined by the characteristics of all the other writers and writings in the system" (368). For Cooper, contextual models serve a taxonomic function; she notes, for instance, that Kenneth Burke's pentad in the *Grammar of Motives* remains valuable for the ways in which it helps label and describe elements of a writing situation but also remains limited because it fails to explain causal relationships (368). Cooper's ecological model asks questions about behaviors and environments, looks for factors that can promote or prevent writing, and analyzes situations and systems to explain or predict change. These are all helpful strategies for evolving WAC programs.

Sidney Dobrin and Christian Weisser (2002) extend Cooper's dynamic model of interlocking systems, particularly in terms of how groups and species shape and are shaped by their surrounding ecosystem and available resources. "Much like the finches and tortoises in Darwin's theory of evolution," they argue, "writers enter into particular environments with a certain ideological code and then contend with their environments as best those codes allow. These environments have material, social, and ideological qualities" (576). As we examine the effects of local environments on writers and writing, Dobrin and Weisser note that the metaphors we use to describe the writing spaces are important (577). Evolutionary metaphors often rely on the image of a radiating network or web. Cooper uses the image to remind us that "anything that affects one strand of the web vibrates through the whole"(370). Dobrin and Weisser also describe "the webbed writing environment" (585) as they focus our attention on activities as well as locations and on the complex ways in which our physical and social environments shape and are shaped by our writing (578).

Cooper, Dobrin, and Weisser focus on writers and texts. I suggest that we extend their theorization of writers as species to theorize WAC programs (administrative units within specific university environments) as species that similarly evolve, adapt, and reproduce. Martha Patton has already begun this work in her insightful book, *Writing in the Research University: A Darwinian Study of WID with Cases from Civil Engineering* (2011). In making a case for an evolutionary theory of WID, Patton is quick to note the limitations of any analogy between biological and cultural processes, but emphasizes its value for "discussion of writing in larger forums of competition (not just within, but also beyond the walls of various disciplines)" and as a way "to explore both variability and stability in writing activity, to consider the impact of environment and its varying constraints on writing activity, and to describe the spectacular radiation of disciplinary specializations" (7). Patton's book-length study articulates and illustrates a descriptive theory that encompasses research, teaching, and administration as she analyzes cases from civil engineering. My aims are different: I want to focus on ways in which evolutionary theory can help us create and apply a heuristic for WAC program administration and self-study.

An Evolutionary Heuristic for WAC Administration and Self-Study

Darwin points to the heuristic value of his work as he concludes *On the Origin of Species*. Starting with the premise that every "production of nature" has a history, Darwin anticipates that: "A grand and almost untrodden field of inquiry will be opened, on the causes and laws of variation, on correlation of growth, on the effects of use and disuse, on the direct action of external conditions, and so forth.... Our classifications will come to be, as far as they can be so made, genealogies" (372). But what questions allow us to study patterns of inheritance, especially in terms of tracing the genealogy of WAC? To what degree can we claim that different species of WAC share common goals for writing, thinking, learning, and knowing even as they adapt to the social, intellectual, and physical elements of their home environments?[2] And what is the effect of environmental enrichment? Too often, we seem to speak in Lamarckian terms where change is rapid, progressive, easily passed along to offspring, and never resulting in extinction. A Darwinian model suggests that change occurs much more gradually over several generations where successful mutation allows an organism to survive and reproduce while failed mutation results in extinction. As Darwin summarizes, "natural selection... only takes advantage of such variations as arise and are beneficial to each creature under its complex relations of life" (95). We see this in the only illustration in *Origin of Species*, the "Tree of Life" (see Figure), where Darwin shows branches extending from a common root. On both sides of the diagram, we see that development is not symmetrical. On the right-hand side of the diagram, in particular, we see how some branches become extinct as others form the main trunk (87).

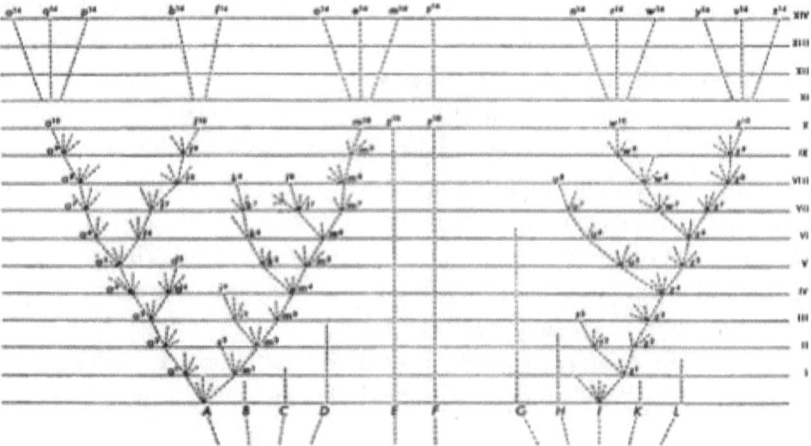

Figure 1 Darwin's Tree of Life illustration, Origin of Species, 1859, p. 87.

Because of its ability to analyze causes for variation, survival, and extinction in a non-linear manner, Darwinian selection and reproduction is a useful model, yet this evolutionary metaphor (like any metaphor) is necessarily limited. It forces a focus on change and physical environments without directly addressing social interactions, ideologies, and enculturation (a point that Condon and Rutz were perhaps trying to address with their metaphor from quantum mechanics). Nonetheless, the evolutionary metaphor can, if used heuristically, provide a structural and conceptual frame for exploring program history, variation, survival, and extinction. It should let us look for common patterns as well as local variations in ways that might prove particularly useful for new or emergent programs where location and momentum have yet to be established.

Such a heuristic for exploring the genealogy and adaptation of WAC programs might focus on the following questions:

1. What *distinctive features* define WAC at your site?
2. What *strategic alliances* establish, support, or advance your program?
3. What *conditions* initiate, develop, threaten, or sustain WAC at your site?

The first question establishes existing structures. Questions 2 and 3 focus on factors that shape change over time.

In the quick sketches below, I will test this heuristic's ability to explore what is ecologically interesting about an existing program's genealogy (its innovations, replication, and survival; or its innovations, endangerment, and extinction). The places where the evolutionary metaphor inevitably breaks down will, I hope, draw attention to the ways in which programs are also shaped by complex social interactions and ideologies, a point I will come back to in my conclusion.

In other words, I am working from the premise that WAC programs do not spring forth fully formed. Some, for instance, may start as an innovation (or mutation) in a single semester when a member of the writing faculty collaborates with another discipline to present a workshop on writing; others may start with some funds from a seed grant or in response to a university assessment initiative. Whether or not something further evolves from that innovation then depends on whether or not it proved successful and whether or not conditions exist for repeating the activity. Changing conditions always drive the processes of selection and replication, generally with the goal of continuation or survival. If an innovation (such as a WAC initiative) survives, then other changes are likely to follow as the cycle continues. The progression does not, however, follow a straight line. That is, some innovations will prove dead ends, some changes will enrich, and still other changes will respond to a completely distinct set of conditions and start a new branch. With an evolutionary heuristic, we can look to long-standing and well-documented WAC programs to trace their genealogies and the adaptive alliances that form along the way.

To test the heuristic for exploring the genealogy and mutation of WAC programs, I am choosing to look at two distinct environments: Carleton College, where the WAC program flourishes within a small liberal arts college setting, and George Mason University, which represents a successful program in the context of a large research university. There are clearly many other long-standing programs that could provide equally compelling cases for study. I am choosing these two for the distinctive ways in which the programs speciated by adapting to assessment requirements (somewhat like looking just at beak adaptations in Darwin's famous finches), and because I was able to augment the richly documented histories of each program (available through existing scholarship and Web-based materials) with site visits where the directors generously allowed me to interview them and see some aspects of their programs in action.

Carleton College: Features, Alliances, and Conditions within a Liberal Arts Environment

Carleton is a highly ranked, private liberal arts college in Northfield, Minnesota, with about two thousand undergraduate students (90 percent of whom live on campus) and 200 faculty. Admissions are competitive with only 21 percent of applicants accepted in 2013. The school's history dates back to 1866. Among other goals, Carleton "strives to be a collaborative community that encourages curiosity and intellectual adventure of the highest quality" with an academic focus on "developing the critical and creative talents of our students through broad and rigorous studies in the liberal arts disciplines" (About Carleton). The size of Carleton helps foster a strong sense of community where colleagues share a common commitment to the value of a liberal arts education. As Carol Rutz, director of Carleton's Campus Writing Program, explains, "They share a belief that communication skills, variously defined, will help students in every aspect of their lives whether it's advancing their learning as undergraduates or helping them succeed in the next phase of their lives. . . . It's there in physics as much as it is in music or history" (Interview).

Carleton's WAC program is most recently documented in the *College Composition and Communication* article that I cited in my introduction. In that article, co-authors William Condon and Rutz (director since 1997) trace Carleton's four-decade progression through the various types identified in their taxonomy. They note Carleton's status as a Foundational Program in the 1970s (366); its twenty-year "limbo" as an Established Program (369); the step to becoming a Type 3 Integrated Program around the year 2000 (373); and the effect of a new curriculum in 2010 that establishes WAC at Carleton as an Institutional Change Agent (Type 4) on the basis of its role in "assessment of student outcomes at multiple sites" as well as WAC's continuing focus for faculty development (378). In other articles that document Carleton's history, Rutz and her colleagues are able to trace the branching progression in more detail. An analysis of the program's genealogy shows, for instance, how WAC at Carleton has become closely allied with assessment even as it maintains its early elements of faculty and curriculum development.

What Distinctive Features Define WAC at Carleton?

As I noted above, the aim of this first question is descriptive. Carleton College is now well known for its use of portfolios to assess students' writing abilities and experiences. Approaches to writing and the teaching of writing have, however, evolved over several decades. Faculty development workshops in the mid-1970s initially supported a change in the way in which undergraduates would meet a campus-wide writing requirement. Instead of taking a single composition course taught by the English department, Carleton students could take a course in any subject that had a "Writing Requirement" (or WR) designation. Rutz, Hardy, and Condon trace this history in a 2002 essay in which they observe that, "the system was distinctive in having replaced a system of instruction with one of certification" (9). They explain that the early stages of the WAC program "rested on the assumption that faculty were already assigning a good deal of writing in their courses across the curriculum; workshops that focused on creating and responding to writing assignments then provided faculty outside of English with the support they needed to offer these WR courses" (8-9). Over time, this innovation has become but one aspect of Carleton's multifaceted program. Interestingly, the 2002 essay uses an evolutionary metaphor to describe cycles and conditions of change. That metaphor, adapted as a heuristic, can help explore not only changes over time in a single program but changes that occur across programs.

For instance, cross-disciplinary faculty workshops were successfully replicated at Beaver College. Elaine P. Maimon credits Harriet Sheridan's "faculty rhetoric seminars" at Carleton College in 1974 and 1975 as the inspiration for organizing similar faculty workshops at Beaver College. Writing in 1990, Maimon observes: "Now that such faculty gatherings have become as familiar as committee meetings, we forget that the faculty workshop was something new in the seventies. . . . [I]t is different in that the workshop is (1) scholarly and pragmatic and (2) politically and intellectually nonhierarchical" (142). It's a good reminder that WAC programs don't emerge fully formed. At Carleton and elsewhere, faculty workshops on the teaching of writing help establish writing as an institutional value that cuts across all disciplines.

What Strategic Alliances Support or Advance WAC at Carleton?

Even within Carleton's writing-rich habitat, WAC depends on relationships and partnerships (co-adaptive alliances in terms of evolutionary theory). When I interviewed Carol Rutz about current conditions at Carleton, she continually brought the conversation back to her colleagues across campus. According to Rutz, the faculty are "completely committed. They are what make it all work." Faculty alliances have, in fact, helped the portfolio assessment model not only survive but replicate.

A symbiotic relationship between WAC and Qualitative Reasoning (QR) began "almost accidentally" when a group interested in improving QR instruction thought to look for examples within the writing portfolios that Carleton students already submit on a regular basis. The Quantitative Inquiry, Reasoning, and Knowledge initiative (QuIRK) found that "by placing QR in the context of argument, we can leverage the assets of the writing program to overcome institutional barriers, develop broad faculty support, and sidestep cultural inertia that plagues new initiatives. And, we argue, all of this can be done while reflecting facets of QR that would otherwise be underrepresented in programming" (Grawe and Rutz 16). One of the initial barriers was funding. Darwin would, of course, remind us that organisms compete for limited resources. By partnering with WAC, the program was able to move forward without a budget line while establishing a critical mass of support. Now that the initiative has found grant funding of its own, it can reciprocate by offering support to writing. Beyond shared funding, the two programs can share another limited resource: faculty time (10). This alliance and replication has proven so successful that other cross-curricular initiatives at Carleton continue to extend the model: librarians at Carleton now have an independent research project that uses portfolios to see how students are using sources (Rutz Interview). Rutz summarizes the advantage of these faculty alliances: "What we all share is a genuine respect for students and a genuine commitment to helping students learn. How we enact that just plays out differently in different disciplines" (Interview).

Continuity for any program depends to some degree on budgets and upper-administration decisions. As a result, administrative alliances also have to be fostered and maintained. Rutz notes that she needs to build and rebuild her relationship with the associate dean position since that role rotates every three years. "For many years," she explains, "I met with the associate dean every two weeks and could drop in as needed. Now I meet once a month and their schedules don't allow for informal meetings. It's harder to build relationships." An alliance with upper administrators matters not only in terms of sustaining current work but also in looking to the future of the program since those alliances will almost certainly shape the transitions and continuity in program leadership. When Rutz was initially hired in 1997 (at a key transition point when the program was shifting its focus from faculty workshops to an assessment-based model), she was in a temporary position that has gradually grown to full-time over the years.

It is now impossible to imagine Carleton's program achieving or maintaining its current status without the support of a full-time director. (The position is currently defined as two-thirds administrative and one-third adjunct teaching.) Rutz notes, however, that while the position is now full-time, it remains limited in at least two ways. Because the position is not tenure-track and is not allied with any department, it is not protected in the same way as a tenured faculty position, which could prove a threat to the position's (and the program's) long-term survival. While the position emphasizes the College Writing Program director's active role as a teacher and thus contributes directly to Rutz's credibility with faculty colleagues, she points out that the position has limited opportunities for curricular involvement or development. The departmental home for the director could, from her perspective, "be Physics as easily as English," but it would give the position "a constituency other than the dean's office" (Interview).

While Carleton's program will certainly continue to thrive as long as Rutz directs it (thanks in no small part to her deep history with and knowledge of the campus culture in addition to her knowledge of and contributions to WAC scholarship), she voices some concerns when asked about how she might manage transitions and continuity in leadership at some future point:

> I don't think it's up to me. . . . My big worry is that cold-hearted administrators facing budget pressures could look at my position and decide that they could get it all covered without replacing me: my teaching could be absorbed by a department, my portfolio work could be absorbed by the assessment office, and my faculty development work could be absorbed by the Center for Teaching and Learning. While the College could get it all covered that way, there would be no leadership model, and—as Ed White has said—having no leadership is risky. There would be no one to pay attention, to do the tending.
>
> Also, finding replacements depends on where you are. Does Carleton know what to look for? . . . Will Carleton have the choices that a place with more visibility or a different location will have? I don't know. (Interview).

Rutz's concern about the future of WAC at Carleton is a concern that may resonate with many directors: despite any program's strong grassroots support, its future may still be determined by budgetary and administrative factors, with decisions made by colleagues who do not have scholarly knowledge of our field.

Studying Carleton's past and present program through an evolutionary lens demonstrates ways in which even the strongest and most well-established programs must continually have someone "to pay attention, to do the tending," to adapt to changing conditions, compete for limited resources, and establish alliances and niches. In addition to needing someone to "do the tending," that someone can't just be anyone. The position requires more than a simple interest in writing; it also requires professional expertise and knowledge of existing scholarship. That is to say, the position of director has become a key feature of WAC as a species. At the risk of stretching the metaphor to the breaking point, directors are a key feature for WAC in somewhat the same way that eyes are a key feature for vertebrates. If WAC were to mutate and become director-less, there is a strong chance that WAC as a species would not only lose programmatic vision but would become extinct (or, barring extinction, WAC might be forced to adapt to a dark and low-energy environment like the eyeless fish in Mammoth Cave).

What Conditions Develop or Sustain WAC at Carleton?

The WAC program at Carleton can now claim a 40-year history. Since long-term change is rarely linear, the innovative workshops that proved to be so important to establishing writing as a core value were not enough to sustain the program without some structural changes. Rutz, Hardy, and Condon cite consistency as the largest challenge (10). They explain that a 1996 internal report on writing revealed that student and faculty experiences within the Writing Requirement courses varied widely. Students noted disparities about the number and length of papers and revisions; faculty noted difficulties in evaluating content versus writing and questioned whether they looked for the same writing skills as their colleagues (10). Because so many faculty were certifying writing requirements in the absence of any common criteria, the certification process also lacked consistency. To adapt to these challenges, Carleton shifted from a faculty-centered approach to one that put students' own writing (and writing selections) at the center. The result: a mid-career portfolio assessment (12). The mutation established a new link between instruction and assessment. Portfolio assessment is now not only established, but starting to replicate in other contexts. In the meantime, faculty development workshops continue to play an important but slightly different role in sustaining campus-wide values.

Rutz and Lauer-Glebov discuss the ways in which one change brings about other shifts in their article, "Assessment and Innovation: One Darn Thing Leads to Another." In particular, they note "a marked change in faculty culture" where instructors take a much more collaborative approach to writing instruction now that "portfolio scoring sessions and other faculty development activities foster continued conversations about students, teaching, and learning" (90). They also point out that the culture is supported with some material resources: "Incentives in the form of stipends, course development grants, and abundant good food have helped strengthen and maintain participation" (90).

While resources do not have to be enormous, they are crucial to a program's survival: they signal that WAC has an established niche. An infusion of funding, for instance, can accelerate change, but there must also be some ongoing support. For instance, initial grant funding at Carleton in 1999 helped create focus and deadlines; the ability to bring highly visible scholars to campus helped forge alliances, gain a national perspective, and spark conversations across campus (Rutz interview). Likewise, steady support such as the continuing appointment of a WAC director and regular funds for faculty development workshops have helped sustain changes over time. As an "institutional change agent" (Type 4 in Condon and Rutz's taxonomy), Carleton's current program may seem fairly secure, but there remains the risk of being subsumed by other innovations. "Writing is assumed as a learning vehicle; it's part of the culture," explains Rutz. "It works so well that it's almost reflex." If anything, the challenge now is to keep faculty aware of the role that writing plays in their teaching so that writing does not become invisible, "like fluoride in the water." The administration at Carleton recently directed a modest bequest to support writing assessment; that decision helps keep the program visible and helps fund its long-term survival (Rutz interview).

WAC speciates by adapting to its local environment; assessment is, for most schools, an environmental requirement. Some species of WAC are better at adapting than others. At Carleton, the portfolios represent a mutation that allowed Carleton to speciate from the proto-species of college writing in general. Co-adaptive alliances emerge as one of the most relevant factors for sustained existence. To explore the ways in which the specific alliances depend on very local conditions, I want to test the heuristic value of the evolutionary metaphor a bit further, first by applying it to a very different institutional context.

George Mason University: Features, Alliances, and Conditions within a Research University Environment

Like Carleton, the WAC program at George Mason University dates back to the seventies. Like Carleton, assessment has come to be an increasingly central aspect of WAC. Like Carleton, Mason's assessment plan is featured on the WPA Assessment Gallery.

Like Carleton, the *US News and World Report* has rated Mason as a top program for writing in the disciplines.[3] Unlike Carleton, George Mason is a large public research university.

The institutional environment at Mason has changed rapidly over five decades. In 1966, Mason was a four-year college with fewer than a thousand students; by

1972, it was an independent university with 4,000 students. By the late seventies (as WAC was getting established), enrollment had already climbed to 10,000. Over the next fifteen years, the size more than doubled to 24,000 by 1996. It is now a major teaching and research university (named the top national university to watch by *US News & World Report* in 2008) with 33,000 students and roughly 1,800 faculty across almost 200 degree programs on three campuses. Due in part to its location in the Washington D.C. metropolitan area of northern Virginia, George Mason University is also characterized by diverse cultures and communities, and 38 percent of its students attend part-time (About Mason).

What Distinctive Features Define WAC at George Mason University?

George Mason University's motto is revealing: "Where Innovation is Tradition" (About Mason). When Mason's WAC program was featured in Fulwiler and Young's 1990 collection *Programs That Work*, Chris Thaiss began his contribution with the simple assertion, "George Mason grows" (223). Thaiss, who directed the WAC program from its beginnings through 1998, witnessed changes in enrollment, staffing, curriculum, and institutional mission. In this institutional context, program survival has relied on continuous adaptation and innovative responses to state mandates and other changing conditions (such as shifts in state allocations of resources). In evolutionary terms, innovation is the key to survival. The WAC program has learned to balance innovation with stability in interesting ways.

The first cross-disciplinary efforts at Mason were (like Carleton's) tied to faculty workshops. The voluntary workshops, held on a weekend, began with some minimal funding from the dean's office. In his 1990 article, Thaiss credits the WAC program's "second major boost" to two state-supported grants: one focused on pedagogy, which allowed the weekend retreats to grow into a five-week institute; the other focused on research and led to a conference and a collection of essays on WAC published in 1983 (224). These twin strands of teaching and publication reflected the shifting institutional climate as Mason worked to establish itself as a serious research university. A third stage quickly followed: a redesign of the English composition requirement in 1983 moved the second required writing course to the junior year with the creation of meta-disciplinary courses that focused on writing in the Humanities, Social Sciences, and Natural Sciences/Technology; a fourth emphasis on writing in business contexts was added in 1986. This emphasis on writing in the disciplines was followed with the Faculty Senate's approval of an additional writing-intensive requirement in the major in the early 1990s accompanied by the creation of a WAC committee (Zawacki interview).

Terry Zawacki succeeded Thaiss as WAC director in 1998. Almost forty years after the earliest WAC initiatives at Mason, faculty workshops, researched publications, and significant writing throughout a student's undergraduate career remain central to the program. In particular, the upper division composition requirement that focuses on four broad meta-disciplines has had an important role at Mason. It puts students from different disciplines together so they can see differences within, between, and outside their own majors (an insight developed in Thaiss and Zawacki's *Engaged Writers*). While environmental conditions at Mason do not support portfolios as Carleton's environment does, these upper division courses serve a similar structural role as a site for assessment (a point I will say more about in a moment).

When asked to highlight the most distinctive features of the WAC program as it exists at Mason today, Zawacki, director from 1998 to 2013, notes "the longevity of the program and the culture of writing it has established." The well-established culture of writing at Mason, she explains, "depends on a large network of relationships" to sustain WAC over time and through changes at the department, college, and university level.

What Strategic Alliances Support or Advance WAC at Mason?

Strong co-adaptive alliances between WAC and other initiatives (such as assessment, national and international research collaboration, or community outreach) can help us understand not only *how* George Mason University created institutional change, but also *why* the program is shaped by its specific environmental conditions. The specific institutional conditions at Mason have shaped writing in ways that suggest that WAC does speciate and diverge from common roots as programs develop features that respond to their local environment.

For instance, assessment is a key strategic alliance for many WAC programs. At Mason, however, assessment of written communication is also a state mandate.

The state mandate represents an environmental requirement that posed both an opportunity and a threat for WAC. On the one hand, it held the potential to strengthen teaching and learning. On the other hand, the state's preference for standardized testing threatened to overlook many important local and contextual factors. Fortunately, writing assessment at Mason had a strong ally in Karen Gentemann, Associate Provost for Institutional Effectiveness. Zawacki credits Gentemann with supporting the writing assessment plan that Mason developed[4] and arguing for it at the state level.

Mason's existing writing-intensive requirement made it possible to keep writing assessment tied directly to courses rather than depending on tests outside the classroom as the state initially proposed. Both the Writing Across the Curriculum Committee and the Writing Assessment Group, a cross-disciplinary committee of experienced WAC faculty convened by Gentemann, worked together to assess the effectiveness of WAC efforts through departmental reviews of randomly selected papers written in response to a representative assignment in upper-division writing-intensive courses and assessed with a discipline-specific rubric. These sample papers were augmented with surveys of faculty and undergraduates. The combined results of this multi-strand embedded assessment process continue to inform ongoing curriculum and faculty development work and the Office of Institutional Assessment has become the main venue for department-level faculty development workshops. This strategic alliance between WAC and assessment is detailed in Zawacki and Gentemann's essay, "Merging a Culture of Writing with a Culture of Assessment: Embedded, Discipline-based Writing Assessment."

This strong assessment model, in place since 2002, faced a new challenge when the Virginia State Council of Higher Education (SCHEV) revised its competency-based guidelines to require institutions to conduct "value-added" assessment (Zawacki *et al*). To be sure that the new state guidelines did not impose timed writing tests or other measures that Mason had already rejected as unproductive, the WAC program needed to defend its successful course-embedded processes for assessing writing over time and in varied contexts; it needed to demonstrate that "writing instruction itself was adding value to students' overall educational experience" (Zawacki *et al*). Again, co-adaptive alliances played a key role in bringing first-year composition (FYC) into the established upper-division WID-based writing assessment process while being mindful of how to make the process productive for FYC curriculum and faculty development.

E. Shelley Reid, the director of first-year composition at George Mason, was able to embed a pre-assessment in the FYC course that considered student writing in the context of upper-division composition courses as well as WID courses. That is, how prepared were students to take advanced writing courses? Reid and her colleagues collaboratively created a rubric that considered several traits according to levels of competency, emerging competency, and consistency. They applied the rubric to 153 randomly selected samples of a single researched essay – a sample that represented roughly ten percent of the FYC student writers (Zawacki *et al.*). The process allowed Reid and her colleagues to consider FYC not only in terms of how it develops students' writing but also in terms of how it prepares them for future writing tasks. Their discussions raised questions about what skills can or should transfer and why transferability is such a complex issue. Reid's discussions resonated with similar conversations that Zawacki had with WID faculty.

For Zawacki, the fact that the majority of the FYC papers in the course-embedded assessment received "emerging competence" as their final score adds quantitative evidence "that all teachers must take responsibility for helping students develop into fully competent writers in their courses, whether in or outside of the major." In addition to these implications for helping students succeed as college writers, the cross-disciplinary assessment process was also important in building and sustaining collaborations and conversations about larger university writing cultures (Zawacki, et al.).

What Conditions Develop or Sustain WAC at Mason?

Survival for any WAC program depends on successful competition for key resources: money, people, and time. Like Carleton, Mason has established itself over decades of work and generations of change.

In terms of funding, Mason's program initially relied on year-to-year allocations from the dean's office and then a series of state grants. It was not until 2001 that the program was given a line item budget from the Provost's office to cover the WAC director's position and workshop stipends. The addition of two graduate research positions in 2005 further expanded and stabilized the budget. The provost recently promised a full-time assistant director (expanding the position from a part-time role), and future plans include a designated space for WAC. As Condon and Rutz note, "substantial, permanent institutional funding for well-defined and established roles and personnel" is one clear sign of a program's institutional importance (362).

Time is a more problematic condition in many ways. One of the George Mason University's institutional goals is to move from being a High Research Activity University to a Very High Research Activity University according to Carnegie standards. That institutional focus can cause a shift in what faculty perceive as valuable. Research universities typically do not reward teaching in the same way they recognize and promote publication and scholarship. WAC director Terry Zawacki explains how this has an effect on WAC: "Many [research faculty] do not want to teach writing intensive courses because they are labor intensive. As a result, we are seeing an increase in the number of adjuncts and term-appointment teaching faculty who are assigned to writing-intensive courses, although the original intent was to have those classes taught by full-time faculty." At the same time that the program is seeing fewer research faculty willing to commit their time to teaching initiatives, the WAC director's research expectations are also increasing: "National ranking depends on external work—publishing, being involved with the Clearinghouse, and so forth. For instance, the fact that George Mason University has been recognized for the past ten years in the *US News and World Report* rankings has helped establish visibility and credibility for our programs in important ways, but it also creates pressure to maintain that ranking" (Zawacki interview). How does a director balance the need to build internal relationships and networks with the pressures to publish? The director's role is, as noted in the discussion of Carleton's program, a key feature of the many species of WAC in various environments.

Another condition for program sustainability depends on planning for continuity. Zawacki poses the question, "How do you value and preserve important institutional history when the initial transition plans didn't work out?" Mason intended to hire their next WAC director while the existing director (Zawacki) was around to provide some introduction and context. That year of overlapping roles proved impossible when the search for a new director took longer than planned. While the program now looks forward to their new director's ideas and initiatives, some institutional history will inevitably be lost despite attempts to create a rich internal archive to augment the ways in which publications already document the program's evolution. Zawacki suggests that all programs consider how to strike a balance between history and innovation. Tracing and preserving a genealogy can help.[5]

Conclusion

An evolutionary heuristic identifies common patterns while also exploring the causes for local variations. It attends to conditions that support or threaten continued survival. By focusing on change and institutional environments without directly addressing social interactions, ideologies, and enculturation, however, the evolutionary metaphor risks placing WAC program directors in a reactive role when what they need is a proactive role that allows them to *initiate* change and *prevent* threats.

That is, the evolutionary metaphor breaks down at a crucial point: there is no intentionality in Darwin's theory. (Polar bears cannot secure their survival in the face of global warming by deciding they need a new way to hunt for food or a new food source.) If I keep extending the metaphor, I suppose I could argue for artificial evolution where humans have recently tried to insert intentionality via genetic mutations (such as gene splicing, recombinant DNA, and so forth). But even this example of intentionality only goes so far. No one can fully predict how an artificially designed mutation will survive and interact within a real environment (i.e., whether it will produce a positive effect such as the prevention of genetic diseases or a negative effect such as antibiotic resistance).

While WAC directors certainly have intentionality and agency, that agency is always and necessarily limited. What happens, for instance, when a new dean or provost no longer supports an existing WAC program? Or when the institutional emphasis on research prompts faculty to withdraw from teaching writing-intensive courses because that work is perceived as less valuable than their publications? Or when students do not see the connections between disciplinary writing and knowing? Competing needs and goals further complicate evolutionary theory. We need to take complex social interactions and ideologies into account to understand the complex history of a program and its potential transformations.

Acting on the premise that complex human interactions can be studied much like any other organism, biologist David Sloan Wilson proposes a theory of cultural evolution that might help us answer questions about agency and competing goals. In *The Neighborhood Project*, Wilson uses examples from biology as "parables" to illustrate successful niche adaptation and poisonous competition (insects that walk on water called "striders") as well as effective collective action (the organization of wasp colonies). He follows these parables with examples of how he and a host of collaborators are beginning to map and study similar processes of adaptation, competition, and collective action in the urban environment of Binghamton, New York. He notes that evolution is "fundamentally about change" and results in a "full spectrum of outcomes" (11). Specifically, he hopes to identify and avoid the conditions that produce individuals who "benefit themselves at the expense of their neighbors" (the striders in his parable) and, instead, identify and promote the conditions that produce individuals who "behave for the good of their groups" (more like wasps) and thus represent "the essence of solid-citizenry" (77). By studying and managing conditions, Wilson contends, the world (or at least his corner of it) can become a better, more cooperative, and harmonious place. The resulting theory of cultural evolution and its goal of producing positive, collective, social action is ambitious and optimistic and yet to be fully proved (the Binghamton project is largely still at the data-gathering stage with only initial, isolated results). Still, Wilson's use of evolutionary science to foster groups that can solve real-world problems shows the analytic value of extending the theory to complex social interactions.

A close study of successful WAC adaptations and evolutions can similarly provide instructive stories to help us examine our own environments with new eyes, attending particularly to ways that our local programs might fill a particular niche or address a particular need through campus-wide collaboration. The evolutionary heuristic that I suggested at the start of this essay works to trace and preserve a program's genealogy, its growth, and its changes over time. It can also provide a way of evaluating where a program wants to go. Close study of both Carleton College and George Mason University's programs specifically identified assessment as an environmental requirement to which each WAC program had to adapt, but also affirmed the importance of a strong and professionally knowledgeable director to build and sustain campus-wide collaborations. As the director of a slowly emerging WAC program, these cases (which were part of a larger, year-long study of several different programs) helped me understand the environmental niche that WAC may and may not fill at my home institution, specifically by looking at available alliances and existing conditions. The initial heuristic has led to more specific questions that my colleagues and I are starting to address as we identify existing strengths and challenges as well as our needs and goals.

Here is an expanded version of the evolutionary heuristic that others may find helpful as they trace the past, describe the present, and look to the future:

1. What *distinctive features* define WAC at our site? Where is writing already happening? What do we know about how faculty *and* students use writing to develop disciplinary knowledge? How do we gain that context? How can we assess whether or not writing develops disciplinary knowledge?

2. What *strategic alliances* establish, support, or advance our program? Where do alliances already exist? What can we do to sustain them? Where should WAC be located to foster new alliances? What do different disciplines identify as their writing needs and goals? How can a partnership with WAC help advance those goals? What is the benefit of a WAC partnership?

3. What *conditions* initiate, develop, threaten, or sustain WAC at our site? Can department-based efforts make a campus-wide difference? Who and what connects WAC efforts across campus? Who is involved? How are the short- and long-term goals decided? Is the process inclusive and consensus-oriented (rather than top-down)? What happens when new administrators introduce new priorities? Or when initial resources (such as development funds) are exhausted? What might celebrate and sustain successful efforts?

The WAC initiative at my university is still very new. We are, like Wilson's Binghamton Neighborhood Project, still at a data-gathering stage and still building alliances as we try to create a successful, cooperative WAC model. Looking closely at existing programs (through site visits, interviews, and publications) was one step in the process. Successful WAC collaborations from one school can never be replicated at another school because of variations in local conditions, but studying existing models through an evolutionary lens did reveal similarities and differences that helped refine our questions for self-study and planning.

A cultural theory of evolution of the sort that Wilson describes is particularly helpful for considering any project that depends, as WAC generally does, on large-scale collaboration. Unlike social Darwinism's emphasis on competition, individualism, and "survival of the fittest" Wilson's theory focuses on group selection and collective action. In fact, Wilson's "parable of the strider" cautions against selfish behavior while his "parable of the wasp" (and the "parable of the immune system" later in the book) clearly favors cooperation. Perhaps Wilson's model also appeals because it implies that prosocial group organisms can control or manage the evolutionary process. I suspect that Wilson's reliance on group selection may remain controversial among evolutionary biologists because of the implied agency, but metaphorically it's a valuable addition: it allows for a proactive role that allows WAC programs to *initiate* change and to anticipate and mitigate threats (even if we cannot always *prevent* them). A WAC program might just secure its survival in the face of budget cuts and shifting priorities by the collective actions of small groups of faculty and students across campus who, connected by well-defined goals and strategic alliances, form symbiotic relationships to practice writing in ways that contribute to their own disciplinary knowledge and to the larger campus-wide culture of writing. In the most optimistic extension of the metaphor, WAC programs become catalysts for accelerating positive educational changes—the very "Institutional Change Agents" that Condon and Rutz celebrate as the most evolved type of program in the taxonomy that inspired this essay.

Notes

I would like to acknowledge the generous colleagues who helped this essay evolve, especially Roy Andrews, Carol Rutz, Tom Sura, Tim Sweet, Terry Zawacki, and the *WAC Journal* reviewers.

1. Cuvier did not believe in evolution. He believed that function alone determined existence and that organisms remained unchanged until a catastrophe caused extinction and the development of a new species. His catastrophe theory seems particularly unhelpful in considering WAC programs.

2. Terry Zawacki and Michelle Cox compile a list of commonly held goals and principles in their work on L2 writers and WAC. See their introduction to the forthcoming collection, *WAC and Second Language Writers: Research towards Linguistically and Culturally Inclusive Programs and Practices* (the WAC Clearinghouse and Parlor Press, 2014).

3. The rating is a result of a strong, existing program in terms of curriculum, faculty, staff, and students, but it is also the result of visibility through local and professional networking as well as national and international scholarship. Only 21 schools nationally make that list; 12 of the schools are public institutions ("Writing in the Disciplines," *US News* 2013).

4. The writing assessment narrative for George Mason University is available online at the WPA Assessment Gallery http://wpacouncil.org/GeorgeMason. It is interesting to compare it to Carleton's narrative, which is also featured as a model: http://wpacouncil.org/CarletonColl. As the head note to each narrative explains: "Together, the White Paper and assessment models illustrate that good assessment [models] reflect research-based principles rooted in the discipline, is *locally determined,* and is used to improve teaching and learning" (emphasis added).

5. Tracing the genealogy of WAC at Mason makes it easy to see why its clear identity, its interdisciplinary policies, and its range of stakeholders would make it a useful example of an established program in Condon and Rutz's taxonomy (Type 2), but it is equally easy to see

how Mason demonstrates their larger point that the taxonomic categories are not mutually exclusive (379). The established structures and supports at Mason, the upper administration's recognition of WAC assessment practices, and writing infused curriculum are typical of Type 2 (Integrated) programs. Mason also possesses the traits of a Type 4 program where WAC is driving change, where the program has substantial permanent funding, where each department is engaged, where WAC is a signature program for the institution and fully theorized, and where multiple campus initiatives coming together to create and sustain a culture of writing (Condon and Rutz 362-63, 274-76). But there is a cyclic, non-linear progression at play, too. The institutional emphasis on research may find Mason once again working to persuade colleagues across campus that writing is everyone's responsibility (Type 1).

Works Cited

"About Carleton." *Carleton College*. Carleton College, 2013. Web. 5 July 2013.

"About Mason." *George Mason University*. George Mason University, 2013. Web. 8 July 2013.

Condon, William and Carol Rutz. "A Taxonomy of Writing Across the Curriculum Programs: Evolving to Serve Broader Agendas." *College Composition and Communication* 64.2 (Dec. 2012): 357-82. Print.

Cooper, Marilyn M. "The Ecology of Writing." *College English* 48.4 (April 1986): 364-75. Print.

Cuvier, Georges Baron. *The Animal Kingdom Arranged After Its Organization: Forming a Natural History of Animals, and an Introduction to Comparative Anatomy.* Trans. and ed. Edward Griffiths et al. London: G.B. Whittaker, 1827. Internet Archive. Web. 4 March 2013.

Darwin, Charles. *On the Origin of Species (1859) and The Descent of Man (1871)*. New York: The Modern Library, 1936. Print.

Dobrin, Sidney I. and Christian Weisser. "Breaking Ground in Ecocomposition: Exploring Relationships between Discourse and Environment." *College English* 64.5 (May 2002): 566-89. Print.

Foucault, Michel. *The Order of Things: An Archeology of the Human Sciences*. New York: Random House, 1970. Print.

Fulwiler, Toby, and Art Young, eds. *Programs That Work: Models and Methods for Writing across Curriculum*. Portsmouth: Boynton/Cook, 1990. Print.

Gladstein, Jill M., and Dara Rossman Regaignon. *Writing Program Administration at Small Liberal Arts Colleges*. Anderson, SC: Parlor Press, 2012.

Grawe, Nathan, and Carol Rutz. "Integrating Quantitative Reasoning Initiatives with Writing Programs: A Strategy for Effective Program Development." *Numeracy* 2.2 (2009): 1-18. Web.

Linné, Carl von. *A General System of Nature, through the Three Grand Kingdoms of Animals, Vegetables, and Minerals*. 1735. Trans. William Turton. London: Lackington, Allen, and Company, 1802. Internet Archive. Web. 4 March 2013..

Maimon, Elaine P. "Beaver College: Getting the Conversation Started." Fulwiler and Young 138-46.

Patton, Martha Davis. *Writing in the Research University: A Darwinian Study of WID with Cases from Civil Engineering.* Cresskill, NJ: Hampton Press, 2011. Print.

Rutz, Carol. Director of the College Writing Program, Carleton College. Personal interview. 8 May 2012.

Rutz, Carol, Clara Hardy, and William Condon. "WAC for the Long Haul: A Tale of Hope." *WAC Journal* 13 (Fall 2002): 7-16. Print.

Rutz, Carol, and Jacqulyn Lauer-Glebov. "Assessment and Innovation: One Darn Thing Leads to Another." *Assessing Writing* 10.2 (2005): 80-99. Print.

— *Carleton Writing Program.* Carleton College, 2013. Web. 1 May 2013. <http://apps.carleton.edu/campus/writingprogram/>.

Thaiss, Chris. "George Mason University: Introduction." Fulwiler and Young 221-28.

Thaiss, Chris, and Terry Myers Zawacki. *Engaged Writers and Dynamic Disciplines: Research on the Academic Writing Life.* Portsmouth: Boynton, 2006. Print.

Wilson, David Sloan. *The Neighborhood Project: Using Evolution to Improve My City, One Block at a Time.* Kindle Edition. New York, Boston, and London: Little, Brown and Company, 2011. E-book. 28 August 2013.

"Writing in the Disciplines." College Ranking Lists. *US News and World Report*, 2013. Web. 28 February 2013.

WPA Assessment Gallery: Assessment Models. The Council of Writing Program Administrators (WPA) and the National Council of Teachers of English (NCTE). 2010. Web. 20 March 2013.

Zawacki, Terry Myers. Writing Across the Curriculum (WAC) Program Director. George Mason University. Personal interview. 16 April 2012.

Zawacki, Terry Myers, and Michelle Cox, eds. "Introduction." *WAC and Second Language Writers: Research Toward Linguistically and Culturally Inclusive Programs and Practices.* The WAC Clearinghouse and Parlor Press. Forthcoming, 2014.

Zawacki, Terry Myers, and Karen M. Gentemann. "Merging a Culture of Writing with a Culture of Assessment: Embedded, Discipline-based Writing Assessment." *Assessment in Writing.* Ed. Marie C. Paretti and Katrina Powell. Assessment in the Disciplines Series, Volume 4. Tallahassee: Association of Institutional Research, 2009. 49-64. Print.

Zawacki, Terry Myers, E. Shelley Reid, Ying Zhou, and Sarah E. Baker. "Voices at the Table: Balancing the Needs and Wants of Program Stakeholders to Design a Value-Added Writing Assessment Plan." [Special issue on Writing Across the Curriculum and Assessment] *Across the Disciplines* 6 (December, 2009). Web. 11 July 2013.

Connecting WID and the Writing Center: Tools for Collaboration

HEATHER M. ROBINSON AND JONATHAN HALL

WRITING CENTER ADMINISTRATORS and scholars have long struggled with the problem of providing useful writing support for students in disciplinary courses, when the tutors who staff writing centers are usually not experts in those disciplines. Writing Across the Curriculum (WAC)/Writing in the Disciplines (WID) programs, for their part, have not always been focused on the specific design of student support, especially for upper-level courses in the disciplines. In this article, we discuss a new approach that we have developed on our campus for providing access to disciplinary knowledge for tutors and students that we call the Discipline- and Assignment-specific Tutoring Tools (DATT). This project has evolved out of collaborations between individuals in our college's Writing Across the Curriculum Program, writing center tutors and faculty members from across the campus, and is designed to help writing center tutors go beyond working on seemingly generic issues in their tutoring sessions to providing directed support for tutor-student collaborations on discipline-specific writing projects. The DATTs address a number of issues identified by tutors, students and instructors, such as the need for concrete models of writing and learning tasks that help students produce writing that conforms to the disciplinary requirements of the field, as well as the need for appropriate interpretation of the assignments and terminology of a discipline or course.

The history of the project we describe here is something like a *Bildungsroman*, in which we set out on a journey that takes both Writing Across the Curriculum and writing center practitioners out of their comfort zones, and hopefully leads us to learn something about the challenges and potential rewards involved. The initiative has been known by various names as it was re-conceived along the way, ranging from "Infosheets" to "Guided Paper Starters," but we have settled on the less-catchy but more descriptive "Discipline-and-Assignment-specific Tutoring Tools" (DATT).

In all of its iterations, the intended purpose was to help close the gap between WAC/WID pedagogy as it is practiced in actual classrooms on our campus, and writing center support services where tutors who were mostly undergraduate and recent graduate English majors were increasingly called upon to tutor outside their accustomed focus on composition and literature courses. The project is also notable for what it reveals about the differing frameworks that underlie WAC/WID and writing center practices.

WAC/WID and the Writing Center: Student Support and Divisions of Labor

The relationship between WAC/WID and the writing center is one of the core topics of WAC scholarship. The current WAC bibliography on the subject lists 233 items ranging from the late 1970s right up to the present (Jory). Writing centers were there at the birth of WAC, and in many cases pre-dated it. Writing Across the Curriculum and writing centers share "intersecting histories" (Mullin), and so the roles of WAC/WID and of writing centers appear to be complementary, with WAC primarily focusing on faculty development, and writing centers on student support. In recent years, there have been calls for a greater integration of WAC/WID and the writing center, with some emerging from the writing center side (Waldo; Corbett and LaFrance) and some from the WAC/WID side (McLeod; Kuriloff). Michael Pemberton pointed out as early as 1995 that in many cases there is a fundamental disparity in theoretical orientation and basic practices between WAC and writing centers, to the extent that bringing the two together, as Pemberton argues, has resulted in an "arranged marriage" founded on "administrative expediency" rather than a core alignment of goals and conceptions.

Because many writing centers arose initially as support for first-year composition, and because most peer tutors have successfully completed that course and many writing center administrators teach it, the issue of course-and-assignment-specific support tends to get submerged in this familiarity. As writing center mandates have expanded to support writing courses beyond composition, issues of discipline have become increasingly important, and yet still tend to fall into the gap caused by the division of labor between WAC/WID and the writing center. The writing center has often operated with the unspoken assumption that student writing is student writing, and that therefore a tutor can approach any session in the same way: by asking the student to provide the context and conventions of the assignment. The tutor's role has been limited to giving feedback as a general reader and as a writing process coach, but it is often precisely the context and conventions that are at the heart of a student's difficulties, especially in highly technical subjects and those with particularly specific rhetorical conventions. The tutor's expertise in supporting composition courses may be of little use here, and might even be counterproductive, if, for example, they advise students to begin by stating a thesis if that is not the usual convention within a given field.

The question of how writing centers should offer tutoring services not only to students enrolled in composition courses but also to those in courses across the disciplines has been a focus of writing center literature for some time. Several scholars (e.g., Hubbuch) have argued that a tutor's lack of knowledge about the content of a specific discipline is both beneficial and appropriate in a tutoring session, whereas others take a more equivocal stance suggesting that some expertise on the part of the tutor is useful in that it leads tutors to direct their sessions towards more higher-order concerns (Kiedaisch and Dinitz). Other scholars argue that disciplinary expertise is necessary for tutoring to have real, long-term value for a client, especially because only an expert can introduce a client to knowledge in the discipline—be it to do with content or discourse conventions—that the client does not and perhaps cannot yet know (Shamoon and Burns; Clark). The consensus seems to be that some disciplinary knowledge is useful in a writing center context, but only when it does not lead to a tutor's appropriation of a client's work. However, the availability of such knowledge in a writing center very much depends on the expertise of individual tutors, often leading to a situation where those who prove to be the best available tutors do not have the disciplinary expertise that would match the needs of students coming to the writing center.

Further, whereas writing centers have often prioritized providing student support over providing specialized preparation for support staff, WAC/WID has not always seen support for students as an integral part of its mission partially because in many cases the writing center was already there when WAC programs got their start and many institutions simply expanded the Writing Center mission to include supporting WAC/WID courses. Overtaxed WAC administrators find themselves with more than enough to do in focusing on their pedagogical training for faculty in WAC pedagogy, and in gradually developing a curriculum that includes writing at every level and in every department. In order to bridge the gap between writing center and WAC foci, we need to find some administrative avenue for addressing the dilemma of a student's experience of college writing. As students move on to more advanced courses, they are expected more and more to mimic and then to internalize and finally to master the genres and registers and conventions of their discipline. They are expected to become members of that disciplinary discourse community, and to learn how to participate in its practices, think according to its epistemological assumptions, and finally write like an insider. If they are having difficulty doing so—and who wouldn't, with so complex a task?—they may seek out support in the writing center.

WAC/WID, Writing Fellows, and the Roots of DATT at York College

York College is a four-year college within a large urban university system, the City University of New York. Our campus is known for its professional programs, ranging from social work to physician's assistant to nursing to medical technology to occupational therapy. As students move from lower-level to upper-level courses, and from WAC to WID, the differing theoretical frameworks of WID and the writing center become more evident. Many of our majors in our "pre-professional" programs must complete writing assignments that focus on highly technical genres that often have strict requirements for producing documents. These genres do not allow for a lot of variation in terms of structure or register, and therefore tutors who have only training in rhetoric or experience in humanities courses will be able to offer only limited advice, if they are to rely only on their own resources.

Our WAC program at York College is a writing intensive (WI) model that is a hybrid of a WAC and a WID orientation. We require two lower-level WI courses, often completed in general education or elective courses, and one upper-level WI within the major. We also required (until Fall 2013), as a prerequisite to all upper-level WIs, a junior-level research writing course that is generally taught by instructors with a rhetoric and composition or English literature background, in which students write a research paper that addresses issues in their field but is framed for a more general audience. One of the signature features of the university-wide WAC program is a major resource: six "CUNY writing fellows"—advanced graduate students who are given WAC training and work fifteen hours per week—are assigned to support the program on each campus. Not to be confused with undergraduate "writing fellows" who tutor at other institutions, our graduate writing fellows usually have significant teaching experience, and can interact with our faculty on a near-collegial level. Their ambiguous positioning within the interstices of the institution—not instructors, not teaching assistants, not tutors, not administrators, yet with elements of each—allows them to serve as intermediaries between all these groups, and this flexibility of role was crucial in both the conception and the development of the DATT initiative.

The courses that we chose for the DATT project were all upper-level courses intended for juniors and seniors, and in one case, graduate students. Within those courses, the DATT project focused on assignments that instructors collaborating with writing fellows had identified as particularly problematic for students. From a WAC perspective, the first question to ask about such assignments is if the assignments are really that difficult or if they are not clearly structured or explained to students. The WAC instinct is to ask faculty to re-think their approach to assignment design and classroom management of assignments. In this case, however, the courses in nursing, occupational therapy, social work, and health education were also courses in which Writing Fellows had been working with the faculty to develop and to implement WID pedagogy by scaffolding longer assignments, using low-stakes and middle-stakes writing and developing assessment tools that include writing goals as well as content goals. These were courses where a lot of effort had already been expended on WID pedagogical design; the DATTs were a natural extension of the work that had already been done.

Designing the DATTs

The DATTs were designed with the following principles in mind, described by the writing fellow who designed the original "Infosheets" template:

> What if we had a kiosk in the Writing Center that stocked an array of one-page handouts with big print and lots of white space, each of which addressed a single very specific writing-related skill? The one-page, big print and white space requirements were important to the concept: if the information could not fit on one side of an 8 ½ by 11 sheet of paper in 14-point type, then it was too much information. Students wouldn't use it, and if they tried to use it, it would be just as likely to confuse them as to help them solve their problem. (Broder 2)

As we started to look at the Infosheets as a resource for the writing center, other benefits became apparent. The format was flexible and open-ended enough so that as long as a writing fellow and a faculty member were interested, there was no limit to the issues that they could try to represent on the Infosheets. Tutors could also participate in the production of these materials by examining them and helping the writing fellows adapt them for the writing center context to help focus the resources on their students' problem areas in a particular assignment or course. The resources could also potentially capture the often-ephemeral workshop material with which tutors are trained, and whose transmission to students was unevenly implemented.

The DATT project arose from the assumption that not all knowledge exists within the student, and that setting up the tutor as an expert sometimes creates false expectations of the tutor's ability to help students with their disciplinary and research assignments. In developing the DATT, we felt that building in structures for collaboration was vital, but as we came to see, each adaptation of the DATT framework raised different issues about the ways in which we ask our students to understand our assignments, and how the writing center staff must be creative in helping the student respond to the assignment in the course of a tutoring session.

The set of DATTs that was designed surrounding the literature review section of the occupational therapy (OT) program's graduate thesis provides a useful illustration of the process surrounding the development of these resources. The writing center's administrative staff had already tried to provide specialized training for tutors to help them negotiate the specialized writing conventions of the literature review. Faculty in the occupational therapy (OT) department had identified this part of the thesis as one that the students struggled with, so the writing center director and a writing fellow met extensively with the OT faculty to develop a workshop to train tutors to understand the conventions of this review so that they could support OT students as they came to the writing center for help. The workshop itself was not particularly effective, however; the writing fellow conducting it had created a lecture rather than a truly interactive experience that would get the tutors thinking about what to do in a tutoring session. The DATT provided an opportunity to revisit the topic with the OT faculty and develop resources with which both the tutors and students could interact. The DATTs stood in for both writing fellow and faculty in explaining how the assignment should be executed. We include the first of the series of DATT for this course here (Figure 1); others can be found at http://www.york.cuny.edu/wac/for-students/discipline-specific-infosheets along with the other DATT resources). This DATT, while more generic than others seen in Figures 2, 3 and 4, shows the basic format of the resources.

The DATTs for this assignment are typical. They begin with a description of the assignment and a description of the conventions that are part of the assumptions of the assignment, such as APA style citations. The DATTs then focus on specific strategies that students might use to successfully negotiate the process of writing the literature review, such as how to read relevant articles effectively, and how to summarize the information that they find in those articles in a way that will make a contribution to the overall focus of their thesis. The DATTs provide a breakdown of the task and the strategies used to negotiate the actual writing of the assignment.

The DATT Development Process: Case Studies

To further illustrate the process of developing the DATT, we turn to the first set that we developed. The starting point for the development of these DATTs was an assessment rubric for the final paper in the upper-division writing-intensive health education course, *Program Planning*. This *Program Planning* assignment was notorious in the writing center. Students would come needing help with their writing, and both tutors and students would flounder to understand expectations for the assignment, and to implement the detailed rubric that the course instructors had developed over the years. When a writing fellow started working with the course instructor one semester on supporting the writing pedagogy surrounding this assignment, the DATTs existed only as a set of generic tools developed to help students with elements of paper writing such as developing a thesis, writing an introduction, and using evidence to support claims. Using the DATT concept, the fellow assigned to the *Program Planning* class developed a set of DATTs to break down the rubric so

---

Writing a Literature Review DATT #1

Writing a Literature Review: Overview

A **Literature Review** represents an in-depth written survey of scholarly articles, books, and other sources in a problem area you choose to research. Your purpose is to substantiate the state of the field: provide an overview of significant literature in your field.

A **literature review**:

- begins with the formulation of a problem or question that you wish to investigate or a hypothesis (an educated guess, hunch, or speculation proposed as a possible solution to a problem that is based on observation and can be supported or refuted through further observation or experimentation).

Example: Chocolate may cause pimples

- addresses why it is important.
- discusses *concepts* and **data**, not "papers", "articles", or authors.
- is *not* a list describing or summarizing one piece of literature after another.
- includes a *critical analysis* of the relationship among different works.
- organizes the significant literature into sections that present themes or identify trends that are related to your research problem.
- does not list all the material published, but *synthesizes and evaluates* according to the guiding concept of your problem or question (your review makes something new out of parts and elements of related articles that you judge as important to your problem or question).
- may be written as a stand-alone paper or to provide a *theoretical framework* and **rationale** for a research study (such as a thesis or dissertation).

York College WAC and Writing Center

Figure 1. Writing a Literature Review DATT #1

students and tutors could interpret it; she worked extensively with a tutor in the writing center to understand the needs and the perspective of the writing center staff, as well as running workshops in the *Program Planning* course with the tutor to help students understand how these resources could help them. Figures 2 and 3 show the first two sheets in the DATT set that supports writing the final assignment in this course.

Program Planning Infosheet #1

Writing a Problem Description

In your grant proposal, you will need to explain to your reader what health problem you are addressing as well as the priority population most impacted by this problem. Your health problem description should:

- Identify and describe the health problem.
- Include relevant international, national, state, and local statistics and data (see DATT #19-20). This research will provide evidence as to the prevalence of your problem and its impact on certain populations. This research will also connect to the next part of the task: your description of the priority population.

Your priority population should:

- Be defined by community. Who does this health problem most effect? Is this group defined by: Age? Race? Behavioral risk factors? Socioeconomic class? Region? Are there any other defining characteristics of this group?
- Be identified by your health problem statistics. Do these statistics support that this group is acutely impacted by your health problem?

York College WAC and Writing Center

Figure 2. Writing A Problem Description (Program Planning DATT #1)

> Program Planning DATT #2
>
> ## Writing a Needs Assessment Plan
>
> ### Methods and Measures
>
> You have identified your **health problem** and your **priority population**, and you have provided your reader with evidence regarding the impact of your health problem at the international, national, state, and local levels, particularly as this problem affects a priority population (see ***DATT #1***). A **needs assessment plan** will now identify exactly what you need to know about this priority population to address this health problem as well as explaining how you will find this information out.
>
> A **needs assessment plan** begins by describing:
>
> - The **priority population** and evidence that this population is impacted by the **health problem**.
> - The **measures** through which you will gain information from this population. For example, will you use focus group questions? Surveys? What other forms might you use to assess this population? You will also need to explain why these **measures** are appropriate for this population.
> - The **methods** through which these **measures** will reach your population. How will you select the focus group, for example? How will you distribute the surveys?
>
> See ***DATT #3*** for the next part of the **needs assessment plan**.
>
> York College WAC and Writing Center

Figure 3. Writing A Needs Assessment DATT (Program Planning #2)

The *Program Planning* case showed how the DATT concept might adapt to disciplinary WI courses. Beginning with instructor documents and input, the writing fellows would break down the process surrounding the writing of a particular assignment in an upper-division course. Having drafted a critical mass of DATTs, the writing fellow would consult with a writing center tutor and revise the DATTs, often breaking the task down further, and creating more of the tutoring tools. Subsequent semesters could see further refinement, but at any stage the DATTs would provide more support for tutors than had been possible in the past. The growth of the DATT project was a real step forward at a college where course instructors were sending students to the writing center, and leaving it to students and tutors to interpret and implement the assignment directions.

The psychosocial assessment assignment from the upper division writing-intensive social work course at York College also shows the utility of the DATT project with respect to supporting WID in the writing center. Of all the assignments in the DATT project, the psychosocial assessment, which is part of an upper-division social work course, is the one that is the least traditional academic assignment. Rather, it is a key piece of writing that many social workers, in a wide variety of settings, use every day in the field. It has in some ways a very rigid structure, yet paradoxically it is adaptable to very different populations and situations. The first of the DATTs for this course is shown in Figure 4.

In the social work case, the DATT project had a lot to work with. The instructor, a former writing fellow, had worked for two years with another writing fellow to develop an elaborate rubric and a workshop for teaching the psychosocial assessment (Oglensky). For DATT, we worked to adapt this rubric, and the materials developed in the professor's *Writing in the Field* workshop series. The DATT documents provided not only a resource for use in the writing center, but also an institutional memory of the WID work involved in implementing the apparatus surrounding the professor's approach to preparing social work students to write the psychosocial assessment. The DATT also allowed us to work against the inherently transient nature of the writing fellows' role at York College, and at CUNY—each fellow is limited to a one-year appointment. The DATTs give us a way to orient new writing fellows to the work that has been happening in faculty collaborations, as well as removing the necessity to reinscribe the pedagogical apparatus every year. The extension into the writing center of this project was, in some ways, an added bonus, allowing upper-division social work students to get support beyond the instructor and the writing fellow assigned to the project as they worked on the assignment. The disciplinary knowledge that the DATT resources encoded would give tutors a leg-up if a social work student arrived in the writing center seeking help.

DATT in the Center: Tutor Roles, Collaborative Training and Realigning Stakeholders

As we have discussed above, at York College there was a real necessity to connect tutors with disciplinary knowledge, and in particular the genres of writing associated with the professional programs in which many of our students major. The DATT resources could help tutors and clients work together, not expecting either of them to be disciplinary experts, but expecting them to be able to make the necessary connections if we provided the scaffolding to do so. The development of the materials has the advantage of being an easily replicable process: the basic format is easily adapted to different assignments and assessment tools, and ongoing collaboration with faculty ensures that the DATT captures both content and pedagogy. The biggest challenge thus becomes making the DATT an integral part of the practice of tutors in the writing center.

Writing a Psychosocial Assessment DATT #1

What is a Psychosocial Assessment?

As a social worker, one of the most important genres of writing you will use in order to convey information about a particular client will be the psychosocial assessment. A **psychosocial assessment** is the social worker's summary as to the problems to be solved. The social worker considers a variety of factors, which may include the physical/psychiatric illness and its impact, results derived from psychological tests, legal status, descriptions of the problem(s), existing assets and resources, the prognosis or prediction of outcome, and the plan designed to resolve the problem(s).

Your **psychosocial assessment** should:

- Communicate pertinent information about a client to colleagues for case planning and referral purposes.
- Establish in writing an account of **"where the client is at"** at a particular moment in time during service provision; the psychosocial assessment account offers baseline information about the client when he or she enters an agency for service.
- Offer the social worker an opportunity to reflect on, refine thinking, and raise questions about the client and his or her situation – to digest information about and impressions about the client through the process of **writing about it**.

York College WAC and Writing Center

Figure 4. DATT #1 for Psychosocial Assessment

From a writing center perspective, perhaps the most disconcerting aspect of the DATT project is that it requires the tutor to take a much more active role in setting the agenda for the session than is customary in many writing centers, including ours. Probably the deepest taboo of the writing center concerns the fear of becoming overly directive. Kenneth Bruffee's classic essay on peer tutoring suggested that too much training could be detrimental. The worst thing for a tutor's self-conception, according to Bruffee, was to be called a "little teacher." Bruffee's idealization of the peer tutor relationship—as two students collaborating on a particular assignment—has been highly influential in writing center theory and practice. Yet in the situations that we are addressing, where the student is enrolled in an upper-level course which assumes a lot of prior disciplinary knowledge, the tutor is not going to be able to collaborate on anything like an equal basis without help. By reaching for the binder that contains the DATT materials, the tutor is making a gesture that suggests the necessity of the instructor's virtual presence in the room that is represented by the materials developed in collaboration between the instructor and the writing fellow. The tutor at this point becomes essentially a part of the instructional team and joins that hierarchy. In writing center parlance, it becomes a *directive* tutoring session—or at least a semi-directive one—where the tutor, assuming the mantle of a surrogate of the instructor, essentially takes control of the session's structure. This was a step that many of our tutors did not feel comfortable making. Therefore it is probably the most important topic to be addressed in the tutor training: how can the tutor introduce the use of DATT—definitely an act of authority to some degree—without leading the student to feel a loss of control during the session?

In theory, given the difference in preparation between tutor and student, the introduction of the DATT should actually help to even things up. The DATT would help maintain "a balance of power," as Pemberton describes it (124), where student and tutor could draw on their strengths with respect to working on a particular assignment, and truly collaborate to produce the type of work that the instructor had explained in making the DATT collection for their particular course. From a writing center/WAC administrator's perspective, the DATT offer benefits beyond providing materials for students to use with their tutors. They provide an opportunity to bridge the perennial gap between instructor and tutor (Carino Floyd, and Lightle; Healy). We take as an ideal Shamoon and Burns's claim for directive tutoring, and adapt it for document-led collaboration. "It allows both student *and* tutor to be the subjects of the tutoring session (while nondirective tutoring allows only the student's work to be the center of the tutoring session)" (145).

The importance of the DATT project from our perspective, however, goes beyond developing a set of useful materials that fill a gap in the resources available for tutors and students in the writing center. The DATT project also illustrates how the relationships between stakeholders in the process of writing disciplinary assignments and the pedagogy surrounding those assignments, were re-conceived in the process of developing these materials, as seen in Figure 5.

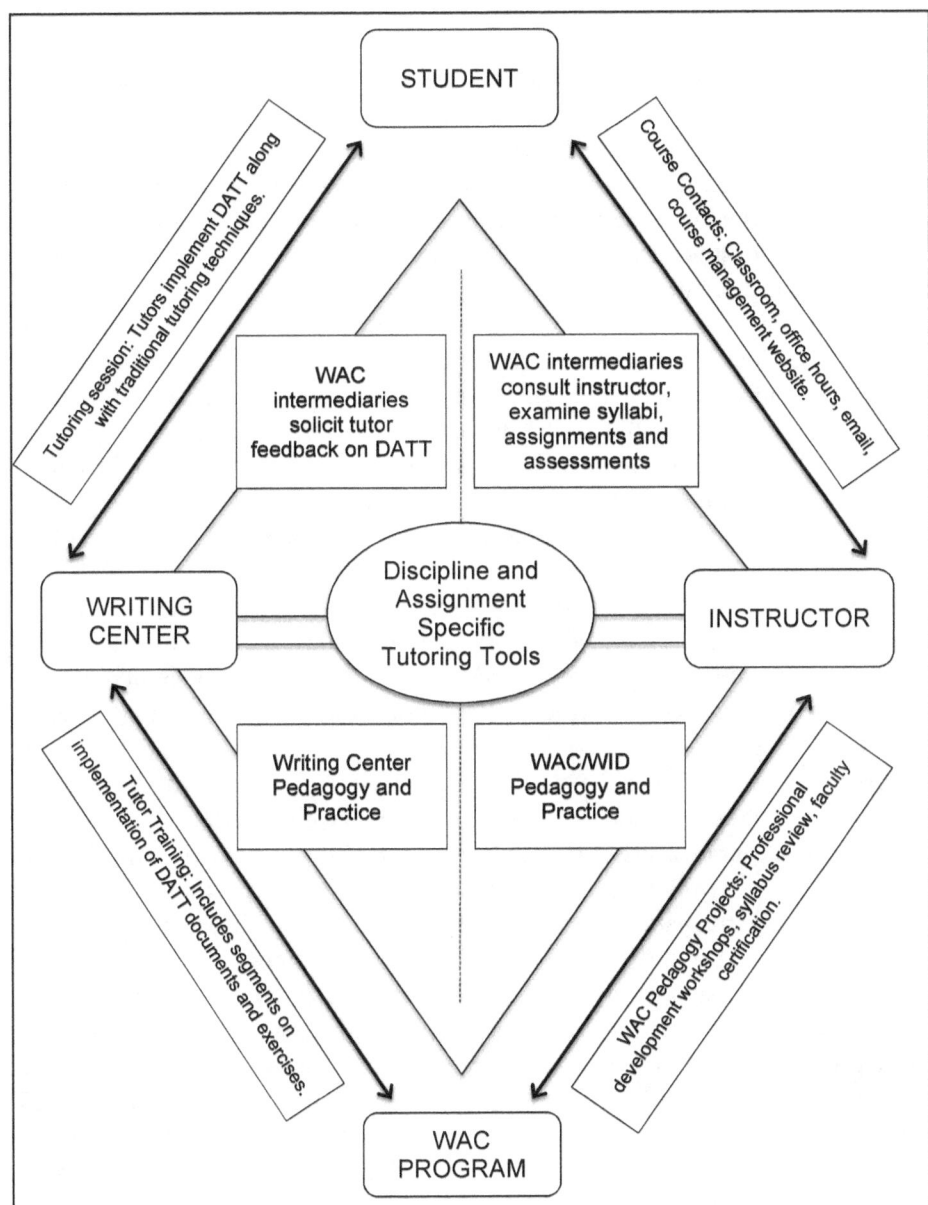

Figure 5. Realigning stakeholders

WAC/WID and the writing center always have a complicated history of interaction; the relationships between tutors, students, and instructors all too often form two lines which meet at only one point. The student and the instructor see each other in class or during office hours, and the student and the tutor meet for their session in the writing center twice a week at most. However, the tutor and the instructor usually do not interact at all. The tutor may help the student to interpret the instructor's intentions based on a written assignment, or the instructor may refer students to the writing center, and may receive a general notification that the student has worked with a tutor after the fact. These methods do not afford an opportunity to fully communicate the genre requirements and specific conventions that instructors are looking for in student writing or in the many possible ways to negotiate content in an academic discipline.

Additionally, Figure 5 illustrates how these relationships were re-conceived in the course of the DATT project. The DATT materials themselves, though very useful as part of a tutoring session, are perhaps even more important as a symbol—and a facilitating condition—of this realignment of shareholders in the academic writing process. They serve as a magnet for activity that helps to close the loop and facilitate communication and collaboration—whether direct or indirect between the constituencies that have often operated independently: a) instructors and tutors, and b) the WAC program and the writing center.

The process of working with the WAC intermediaries compels the instructor to re-conceive the audience for class materials, to repurpose classroom materials for the new context of a writing center session, and to think consciously about designing support for a course—as opposed to just "sending" students to the writing center. In this new conception, there is no more just "sending" a student with writing problems somewhere else; rather, the instructor, through DATT, becomes a participant in what happens when the student arrives and sits down with the tutor.

The WAC Program also becomes indirectly part of that session, not only through the agency of the WAC intermediaries in the process of DATT development, but also through active participation in the process of tutor training. The writing center still conducts its usual training by focusing on the writing process, basic writing pedagogy and the ethics and procedures of general tutoring, but the WAC Program also contributes to this curriculum by incorporating a discussion of basic WAC/WID principles: writing to learn, disciplinary communities, and scaffolding assignments to facilitate learning, in addition to specific training in how to use particular DATT materials created to support specific assignments and courses. These sessions may be run by the WAC intermediaries (such as our writing fellows), by the WAC administrator, by the writing center director, or even by the faculty from DATT-targeted courses themselves, depending in all cases on time and availability. The DATTs make possible support of multiple disciplinary genres, but WID-based tutor training should go beyond the particular models to familiarize tutors with some basics of the disciplinary cultures that produced them (Walker 37). How do practitioners in a particular discipline think? How do their discourse conventions reflect epistemological assumptions about what counts as evidence?

Some Final Thoughts

We see a great deal of potential in the DATT model as a frame for faculty-fellow, fellow-tutor, and tutor-student collaboration, offering students consciously designed support in their WID courses. By bringing the WAC Program into the writing center in a collaborative manner, we work to overcome the traditional division of labor between faculty development and student support. For instructors, the potential use of DATTs in the writing center serves as a useful prompt, a tool for imagining audience and purpose as faculty and writing fellows collaborate on developing materials for supporting specific courses and assignments. Some instructors have begun to make use of the DATTs in the classroom by taking the original resources developed with the writing center in mind, and adapting them for the classroom context. One instructor, using York College's upper-division writing and research course as a laboratory for the use of the DATT, worked with a writing fellow to incorporate exercises into each sheet. The absence of the tutor meant that the DATTs themselves needed to be more directive. We provide two examples showing these exercises in the Appendix. Once again, the input of individual faculty members in the process of customizing the DATTs for individual classrooms is essential. Leaving the development of exercises solely to the writing fellow, as this instructor quickly discovered, led to overly general exercises that relied on texts from outside the course. Since this writing course is already reading-intensive, adding more reading that was outside the specific focus of the course would have quickly built resistance from the students.

As we continue to link WID and the writing center, we will assign a writing fellow to the writing center for several hours a week to provide support and do ongoing assessment of how the DATTs are used, and what resources need to accompany them so that they can work better. We will track how many students from targeted classes attend the writing center, and how frequently the DATTs are used in the writing center when they do. We will survey both instructors and students about their perceptions of the effectiveness of the materials and of their students' interactions with tutors.

In potentially expanding development of such tools to other campuses, the key elements would be to:

1. Make use of a compensated intermediary. In our case we were fortunate to have writing fellows already on staff to fill this role, but on other campuses various mechanisms could be used. Tutors could work on special projects full-time or adjunct faculty could be compensated by grant money or other resources.

2. Limit the impact on a faculty member's time by making use of materials already developed (e.g. rubrics) that might be based in consultations between faculty and intermediaries.

3. Make sure that tutors involved in the development and editing of the materials are compensated for their time and have frequent opportunities to offer feedback and to field test the materials in the writing center.

This interactive, team approach respects the different roles that tutors and instructors have in relation to students, but it finds ways that they can work together through the mediation of the writing fellows. It provides an important mechanism through which the tutor and the instructor, as two professionals engaged in the common task of helping the student to succeed in the course, can coordinate their efforts, and work together for the benefit of their students' writing.

Note

The DATT project that this article explores is the product of many people's work. We would like to acknowledge the contributions of the writing fellows who developed the DATTs that we show here: Laurel Harris (program planning), Janice Capuana (occupational therapy), Alberto McKelligan (social work), and Elizabeth Alsop / Jack Spear (Writing 300). Laurel Harris also played a significant role in editing the initial manuscript. We also thank the participating faculty and the tutors and staff at the York College Writing Center, for their ongoing contributions to the project.

Works Cited

Barnett, Robert W., and Jacob S. Blumner, eds. *Writing Centers and Writing Across the Curriculum Programs: Building Interdisciplinary Partnerships*. Westport, CT: Information Age Publishing/Greenwood, 2008. Print.

Broder, Michael. "The York College WAC Infobase: A New Resource for WAC-Writing Center Collaboration." Mid-Atlantic Writing Centers Conference. York, PA. April 28, 2009: 1-4. Presentation.

Bruffee, Kenneth A. "Peer Tutoring and the 'Conversation of Mankind.'" *Landmark Essays on Writing Centers*. Ed. Christina Murphy and Joe Law. Davis, CA: Hermagoras Press, 1995. 87-98. Print.

Carino, Peter, Lori Floyd, and Monica Lightle. "Empowering a Writing Center: The Faculty Meets the Tutors." *Writing Lab Newsletter* 16.2 (1991): 1-4. Print.

Clark, Irene L. "Collaboration and Ethics in Writing Center Pedagogy." *Writing Center Journal* 9.1 (1988): 3-13.

Corbett, Steven J., and Michelle LaFrance. "From Grammatical to Global: The WAC/Writing Center Connection." *Praxis: A Writing Center Journal* 6.2 (2009): n. pag. Web. 22 May 2013.

Healy, Dave. A Defense of Dualism: The Writing Center and the Classroom." *Writing Center Journal*, 14.1 (1993): 16-30. Print.

Hubbuch, Susan M. "A Tutor Needs to Know the Matter to Help a Student With a Paper: ___ Agree___Disagree___Not Sure" *Writing Center Journal* 8.2 (1988): 23-31. Print.

Jory, Justin. "The WAC Bibliography: WAC and Writing Centers/Learning Centers.". 22 May 2013. Web.

Kiesdaisch, Jean, and Sue Dinitz. "Look Back and Say, So What?" The Limitations of the Generalist Tutor." *Writing Center Journal* 14.1 (1993): 63-74. Print.

Kuriloff, Peshe C. "Writing Centers as WAC Centers: An Evolving Model." Barnett and Blumner, 105–18. Print.

McLeod, Susan H. "The Future of WAC—Plenary Address, Ninth International Writing Across the Curriculum Conference." *Across the Disciplines* 5 (2008). Web. 2 June 2013.

Mullin, Joan. "Writing Centers and WAC." *WAC for the New Millennium: Strategies for Continuing Writing-Across-The-Curriculum-Programs*. Ed. Susan H. McLeod, Eric Miraglia, Margot Soven, and Christopher Thaiss. Urbana, IL: NCTE, 2001. 179–91. Print.

Oglensky, Bonnie D. "Record-Keeping and Professional Socialization in Social Work." *International Journal of Interdisciplinary Social Sciences* 3.6 (2008): 7-14. Web. 2 June 2013.

Pemberton, Michael. "Rethinking the WAC/Writing Center Connection." *Writing Center Journal* 15.2 (1995): 116-34. Print.

Shamoon, Linda K., and Deborah H. Burns, "A critique of pure tutoring." *Writing Center Journal*. 15.2 (1995): 134-152. Print.

Waldo, Mark L. "The Last Best Place for Writing Across the Curriculum: The Writing Center." *WPA: Writing Program Administration* 16.3 (1993): 15–26. Print.

Walker, Kristin. "The Debate over Generalist and Specialist Tutors: Genre Theory's Contribution. *Writing Center Journal* 18.2 (1998): 27-45. Print.

Appendix: DATTs from the Research Writing Course

Writing 300 DATT #3

WRITING A SYNTHESIS: TOPICS & THEMES

Your professor will assign sources for you to read. They may be newspaper or scholarly articles, essays, excerpts from books, or another type of source.

The **topic** is the general subject of your reading. Examples of topics include advances in medical technology, climate change, or the causes of the Civil War. **Themes** are more specific. Although your source has only one topic, it may contain multiple themes that relate to this topic. For example, a source on the topic of drug addiction may deal with the following themes: the consequences of addiction, the science of addiction, treatment options for addicts, etc.

Most General   *Most Specific*
Topic --------------> Themes --------------> Ideas

Note: Instead of "themes," your professor may ask you to identify "ideas," "sub-topics," or "main points"—all mean roughly the same thing.

As you read your sources, keep in mind the following questions:

- What is the topic of the reading?
- Read the title. What does it suggest? As you read through the source, try to determine what the author is focusing on.
- What key ideas or themes related to this topic are discussed?
- Are there any particular ideas to which the author repeatedly refers? What are these? Are there any related ideas (or themes) to which the author refers? Why might the author refer to these?
- What does the author say about these themes? Why might the author provide these ideas about these themes?

Remember that you will need to re-read your sources several times. The first time, you may want to scan quickly for the topic and main ideas. The next time, you will need to read more carefully, annotating as you go. You may also want to read sources for a third time, keeping an eye out for common themes.

Exercise: Have students re-read an article that they have been using in class. While reading, ask students annotate the article with the words "topic" and "theme" next to sentences where they see these emerging. When the article is annotated, students can work in groups to answer the questions in the bullet points above.

York College WAC and Writing Center

Writing 300 DATT #4

WRITING A SYNTHESIS: SYNTHESIS VS. SUMMARY

In this paper assignment, you are being asked to synthesize, not summarize.

To summarize means to restate, in your own words, the content of one reading. Summaries are usually shorter than the original reading, and provide the reader with the main ideas of a particular reading. On the other hand, to synthesize means to restate and *combine*—again, in your own words—the content of *more than one* reading.

A summary is a restatement, in your own words, of the main points of a particular reading. A summary is typically shorter than the original reading, and provides the reader with the main ideas of the reading. It does not contain the opinions of the writer, or information on how the reading relates to other, related readings. Also remember that while the organization of a summary tends to follow the structure of the original source, the organization of a synthesis is determined by the writer.

- For example: You might summarize what one article argues about the impact of the Great Depression in the rural south. But in a synthesis, you would include multiple perspectives and arguments from several articles on the same topic.

Exercise:
Write summaries of the introduction of two articles that you have read in class. When you are done, share your summaries with your group, and ask your peers to choose a part of your summary which is particularly effective (one or two sentences). Discuss what makes it effective. When you are done choosing a section from each student's summary, go to the chalkboard and write the sentences there.

York College WAC and Writing Center

WAC/WID Meets CXC/CID: A Dialog between Writing Studies and Communication Studies

DENISE ANN VRCHOTA AND DAVID R. RUSSELL

Introduction

WE WORK IN THE SAME ENGLISH DEPARTMENT doing the same kind of work—but in two very different fields. Here at Iowa State University (ISU), English includes Speech Communication and Communication Studies. We sat down to have a coffee, find out what we have in common (and do not), and speculate about the future.

Writing- and Orally Communicating-to-Learn

David R. Russell—You and I have been doing similar work here at ISU—helping faculty in the disciplines develop assignments, researching their uses of communication in teaching, but we haven't talked much about specific differences in our traditions. The slogan that people have used and debated now for forty years in WAC/WID is "Learning to write, writing to learn," since WAC/WID is really about the relationship between writing and learning. But I don't know how relevant that is to Speech Communication and Communication Studies.

Denise Ann Vrchota—"Learning to communicate, communicating to learn" was a motivation for the people at Central College to launch their CXC program in 1976 (Cannon & Roberts, 1981), and the phrase has been used as an argument for disciplinary support of a more widespread scope by others such as Cronin, Grice, & Palmerton (2000). Can it be justified as a pedagogical approach? Intuitively, yes. If you have students in communication class (or history or whatever) communicating orally, do they learn? Yes. But I say "yes" not as a result of research conducted in communication, but from the results of approaches to learning such as the learner-centered approach and related approaches such as cooperative learning, active learning, reflective learning, and so on. These focus more on communicating to learn compared to work done in the Communication discipline.

DRR: "Communicating to learn" and "writing to learn" sound similar, but the concept of "writing to learn" was developed specifically for the medium of writing, as distinct from oral communication. And isn't "speaking to learn," in a sense, kind of a truism? In a face-to-face classroom, isn't oral communication necessary for teaching? And speaking seems like something that doesn't need to be taught except for special cases, such as delivery of "formal" presentations, or to special populations who need speech therapy. So couldn't improving oral communication be thought of as another way of saying "improving classroom teaching"?

DAV: Perhaps your comment is dependent on the definition of communication. What I have learned from my Communication in the Disciplines (CID) research, which identifies perceptions of communication in other disciplines, is that faculty all too often don't think of what they are doing in class as communication. For example, a faculty member describing to students the circumstances in which they will need to be able to work in groups or on teams as practicing professionals, and how they will do that, that's all about communication. That's teaching communication. And students must be able to translate their technical knowledge so that members of other professions can understand that knowledge, or present it so as to disagree with those in authority. That also is communication. How do students learn to participate in complex interpersonal or group interactions? If communication is the process of working toward shared meaning or a common understanding, how do they get better at it? In Communication, we have courses in this process, which is valuable to students in all the disciplines.

DRR: I guess I was buying into the stereotype of communication as something natural, not teachable. And ironically, it's a similar stereotype to the one I hear many faculty in the disciplines express about writing. The "good" students know how to write. It doesn't need to be taught, only remediated. Or faculty claim writing is not something that can be taught, except for elementary grammar, spelling, etc.

But then I recall that Antonius in Cicero's *De Oratore* also argued that public speaking can't be taught, that it's a gift or knack just picked up.

DAV: Most everyone seems to equate the field of Communication with public speaking, don't they? For me it's ironic because most people in their careers don't do a lot of public speaking, at least in comparison to the amount of time spent in classrooms to teach them and to practice doing it. But it's really difficult to convince individuals beyond the Communication discipline that a body of theory, research, and teaching practices exists that go beyond presentations. Interpersonal, organizational, group, intercultural, gender, nonverbal, computer-mediated communication—everything except written—one might say. So we have something to offer teachers in all the disciplines.

DRR: Communicating to learn?

DAV: Most pedagogical research in Communication Studies focuses on students learning about the communication process as applied to various contexts, usually professional. But there is research that focuses on interpersonal or group communication or even presentations such as lectures in terms of how they influence learning in educational settings. So you have a study of "Relational turning point events in college teacher-student relationships" that looks at teacher-student communication and learning regardless of the discipline, or "a review of research on humor in educational settings" to say what researchers have learned about how teachers using humor in their communication help students learn. But I'd say that researchers in the field of Education rather than Communication have done more to study the role of communication in learning. It is my impression that "writing to learn" is a more immediate concept to WAC/WID researchers and practitioners. Is that accurate?

DRR: Maybe for WAC/WID practitioners. But I don't think so for researchers. Much of the research in writing to learn has been done in psychology or educational psychology, just as you say it has been done in educational psychology for communication and learning. If learning is defined as absorbing content, then writing doesn't seem to have much effect on that kind of learning. But if learning is conceived in more complex terms, then there does seem to be an effect. But again, this is research mostly from educational psychology, not from WAC (Klein, 1999).

And there really hasn't been much theorizing of Writing to Learn since Britton (1975) and Emig (1977) in the 1970s—until about five years ago (Russell, 2012; Russell and Cortes, 2010). Bazerman (2009) and others have been developing the theory around genre. The genres of a discipline, conceived in terms of social action and not just their formal linguistic features, are a way of organizing the thinking and learning—the epistemology and methods—of each discipline differently. So genres might provide a scaffolding for learning. And this might be true of non-written or mixed mode genres, too.

DAV: Lee Shulman, a founder of Scholarship of Teaching and Learning (SOTL) (1987), discusses something he calls "pedagogical content knowledge." He defines it as a "special amalgam of content and pedagogy" (p. 8). I interpret that as meaning that pedagogy is site specific. If that is correct, the site-specific pedagogy of the communication discipline would include much of the disciplinary content.

DRR: That sounds like the "didactics of writing" research in Europe and Latin America, where they study the particular ways a discipline's knowledge (or writing) is—and can better be—formulated for teaching it. A crucial point is that if writing has an effect it's not general. Certain genres or ways of writing are conducive to learning certain kinds of content or learning in certain ways.

DAV: I agree that we need to look at the specific ways writing and speaking are used, and in what particular contexts—that is a foundational principle of CID. So it's very much the context of the speaking/writing that determines or influences whether and how much Writing To Learn or Speaking To Learn goes on.

DRR: Like in the big Open Dialog project (Nystrand, Gamoran, Kachur, & Prendergast, 1997). Researchers found open dialog, as opposed to the typical teacher-structured discussion —interrogation, response, evaluation—was highly correlated with learning, even though the average class engaged in less than one minute of it a day.

DAV: Good class discussion and learning are aligned. No doubt about that. And for learning literature, apparently open discussion is better than recitation, and I would guess it is better than lecture also. What we say is that a competent communicator is one who is able to identify his/her goals, has the ability to assess a situation, and can respond to the needs of a situation as a result of his/her knowledge about communication. Another way to explain this process is to apply the "tool kit" metaphor. The competent communicator has enough communication tools in the kit that he or she is able to select the best one for the needs of the circumstance based on his/her goals. It's a synergism of knowledge and critical thinking. And I see that as consistent with a more broad definition of learning, that individuals do not simply "have" knowledge but that they are able to "use" or "manage" that knowledge.

So, in a broader sense, are there particular ways that writing can, in context, support learning?

DRR: Writing to learn theory has pointed to several ways writing supports learning in contrast to face-to-face (usually oral) communication—not that writing can't be face-to-face, as with passing notes in class. But writing can materially cross time and space. Documents are, in the phrase of Bruno Latour, "immutable mobiles" (1990), allowing a kind of reflection, and recursive composition, that is impossible with oral communication (unless it's recorded on some material—tape, silicon—and materially manipulated). One can construct a text spatially and move words and other signs around on it. As C. Day Lewis is reported to have said, "How do I know what I mean until I see what I say?" And writing can stay forever, given the right technology (ignoring shredders and acid paper and fire and so on). So it has more potential to influence—for better or worse.

So, let me ask you the same question. What are the particular ways that speaking can support learning?

DAV: With oral face-to-face, you have to think on your feet. Lying is harder. That supports learning. And you can more quickly with speaking establish a relationship, create common meaning, than with a written exchange over time. Modern science started with scientists visiting each other's labs to witness experiments and talk, face-to-face. But as scientific study grew, a written record became necessary. Still, I could paraphrase C. Day Lewis, "How do I know what I mean until I hear what I say?" The act of talking can be a powerful way to learn. Discussion is a way of co-constructing knowledge and understanding. It is ancient dialectic, as with Plato.

DRR: I'm not clear on what the difference between CXC and CID is.

DAV: The field is now known as Communication, formerly known as Speech or Speech Communication and includes Communication Studies and Rhetoric. CXC or communication across the curriculum is the name given to programs that serve students and faculty in other disciplines with communication activities. CID refers to communication in the disciplines and is the research term for individuals who study the communication traditions in other disciplines.

DRR: So what shall I say you teach?

DAV: Communication.

DRR: But written communication is communication.

DAV: Let's just call my field Communication (capital C) and yours Writing (capital W). Communication, as I mentioned, includes research on nonverbal (non-oral) communication. But we can agree that at some level it's all rhetorical.

DRR: Indeed! But we've immediately got complex categories and territories to understand—and perhaps negotiate.

DAV: As you know, the Communication discipline has been based on something we call "the basic course," which would be the counterpart to your First Year Composition (FYC). The basic course for many years was a traditional public speaking course required of most undergraduate students. The traditional public speaking basic course usually means that students give three to five major speeches during the term. A survey of the textbooks for this course over the years shows remarkable stability in the concept of the public speaking basic course. But in the 1970's, another type of basic course was added in some institutions, known as "the hybrid course." In addition to public speaking, it also contains instruction in interpersonal communication and sometimes small group work—all of which is useful in CXC/CID. And since the late 1980s, we've had Communication Centers, where students (and faculty and others) can film their speeches and receive feedback, usually from a peer tutor (Yook & Atkins-Sayre, 2012).

DRR: I didn't know that the basic course came in two types, the traditional and the hybrid. In Writing, textbooks also show remarkable continuity in composition courses. But I suppose the biggest change in writing instruction since the 1970s is the process movement, where we began teaching and researching the processes of writing as well as the products. That had big implications for WAC/WID practice and research, because we're not just about the form of writing, which is what concerns most applied linguists, but also its relation to the knowledge—and know-how—of the disciplines, and the informal writing that goes on, or can.

By the way, would you say writing is taught in Communication courses?

Writing to Speak

DAV: Communication teachers do require a lot of writing, but whether writing is explicitly taught in a communication classroom, I'm not sure. In my own classes, the extent of my writing to speak action would be spending time in the classroom explaining the requirements and the "why" of my written assignments: "I'd like you to describe _____ because _____." As you said earlier, a central goal of writing is to evaluate learning. Much of this is practical. Writing is more efficient for gathering assessment data—and makes it less likely that nerves or a bad day will skew performance, in comparison to speaking.

Oral activities or exercises are a part of the knowledge acquisition process in some classrooms but rarely do the students' grades depend entirely on these. For example, in a public speaking class the outline probably counts toward the grade as well as the speech. So the display of knowledge on paper coupled with the possibility that they do or do not do something they should when speaking assumes a more complete picture of the students' abilities. I think the same could be said for the balance of written and communication activities in an interpersonal or other non-presentation class.

It almost seems that in the Communication discipline—as well as others—what is spoken counts less.

DRR: Ah, yes. Writing is more highly valued in the culture than speaking, more "real" in some senses but not in others. In some cultures university students have high stakes oral examinations (Italy, for example), "in vivo," because then their professors can probe their knowledge in dialogue. That was true in the US until the 1870s, when written exams became the norm and—not coincidentally—written composition began to be taught.

But do communication teachers use writing for learning in addition to writing for assessing learning?

DAV: One practice in communication classes is for students to write a series of fairly brief (two-page) papers in which they apply disciplinary concepts to their personal experiences. In addition to "learning the material" and practicing its application, the papers encourage thinking and students' identification as a communication scholar.

DRR: Doing brief and informal writing repeatedly, over a period of time, tied to the activity of the class, is really central to WAC/WID approaches, as is writing for reflection, as your writing activity does (Bean, 2011). And actually quite a number of writing-to-learn activities that are common in WAC/WID practice are, in a sense, writing-to-speak activities, like a written response to a question about the reading or an answer to a question posed the previous class period. These are ways of preparing students for the classroom discussion to come. The same might be said for a brief written brainstorming activity before a discussion. One might also have students write down their goals for a group project and then share those in a first group meeting as a way to clarify and/or resolve differences before beginning work.

But what about formal writing to speak? You mentioned outlines.

DAV: As a founder of the field of Communication, James Winans quipped, "A speech is not an essay standing on its hind legs." But in public speaking classes, emphasis is given to the construction of outlines as a means of clarifying the main points the speaker wishes to make, ensuring that main points are developed in consistent fashion. And in interpersonal and group communication, writing is a way of structuring as well, and a way of learning together. In a committee meeting or job performance interview people can't always present themselves spontaneously without embarrassment, but they can anticipate and compose some talking points or notes. Meeting notes and minutes structure future meetings. And all of these techniques can apply to working in disciplinary classrooms, especially in the applied sciences.

DRR: I'm thinking historically now. For the first twenty-two centuries after the Greeks founded rhetoric, writing was used mostly as preparation for speaking. Writing was a heuristic device. It's part of finding something to say and organizing it. You make notes of various kinds, and organize them into an outline, then you write your speech out and memorize it. The canon of delivery! That's the classical model, right? Up until the 1870s in US colleges, writing was mostly for preparing to speak, an incidental and invisible part of the rhetorical curriculum. My point is that writing to speak was the story of rhetoric for all those years. So we're in a different world now. A world of new media mixing the modes. And in this age of electronic recording, all or almost all of the material affordances of written communication are available to recorded spoken or video. A politician's every recorded word crosses time and space, is analyzed, and he or she is made to account for it.

Do you see this affecting Communication pedagogy? For example, students videotaping themselves beyond their public speaking?

DAV: Yes, videotaping is used but can be beneficial across the board, not only in public speaking. You videotape two people talking to each other or a group working and when the participants view themselves, their view of what happened during the interaction is often different from what they thought was happening when they were participating. It's a great way to learn. But the other goal besides the reflective experience is to figure out a way to help students see the importance of having a kind of out-of-body experience whenever they engage in communication—they need to become their own camera. Sometimes people don't realize they just talked for fifteen minutes about something that had nothing to do with the meeting or they didn't see the dismayed or supportive facial expressions of their colleagues when they proposed a motion. One goal of communication is to help people narrow the distance between the way they see themselves and the way others see them. Communicating with a wide lens and big ears is really important to achieve that goal.

Speaking to Write

DAV: So, how about speaking to write?

DRR: Speaking to write? Well, James Britton theorized writing-to-learn and writing across the curriculum in the 1970s, and he was very much interested in what he called "talk," something like open dialogue (1975). But although that became an important concept in UK secondary school teaching, that wasn't specifically developed in US composition, perhaps because of the writing/speaking divide we've been exploring.

However, there's a fairly long and strong tradition in composition, going back to the 1980s, certainly to Kenneth Bruffee (Kail, 2008), of small group discussion to aid in generating ideas. But that's been theorized not in terms of Communication but in terms of collaborative learning. In fact, Bruffee's major work is called "Collaboration and the Conversation of Mankind" (1984). The idea is that collaboration, oral and written, and oral is key in his view, can improve writing and learning.

And before that, a central tenet of the whole turn towards process, the writing process movement, was revision based on feedback from peers, of peer-to-peer and small group revision feedback. It might be called "speaking to revise," though I don't know that it ever has been.

And before that, writing centers were and are very much based on a pedagogy of face-to-face interpersonal oral communication. But again, I don't know of anyone calling it "speaking to write."

What do you think we writers could learn from Communication that might improve our speaking-to-write?

DAV: A writing instructor who implemented group activities could learn and apply Communication theory to social and task functions of a group. And types of groups. And member roles.

And Communication research has developed several systematic heuristics sequences that might be applicable to working groups in writing classes. There's "functional perspective of group decision making" developed by Gouran & Hirokawa (1983) and classical stasis theory developed by Infante (1988). Using any of these structures might initially seem awkward when applied to a writing assignment, but I can see that any of them could be used to guide the discussion so the author of the assignment would have some ideas about what to do next.

CID/WID Research

DRR: WID has been about research writing in the disciplines, scientific writing, mostly, though the research writing in most of the humanities has been analyzed, too, because research writing is so powerful in our society. It's the way new knowledge is officially made. By being put into writing.

DAV: I agree that written publication makes knowledge official. But generating knowledge is very much dependent on oral communication. Long before the publication process, even before the first draft, there is group process in the labs. Beyond the group dynamics of the lab, there are oral presentations, oral feedback, hall talk, and so on.

DRR: I see that. But do the genres of group, interpersonal, and presentational communication differ among disciplines?

DAV: Indeed! In some disciplines and professions, a discipline-specific oral communication genre is at the very center of its practice, of its value. Design presentations, called "critiques" or "crits," are the fundamental pedagogy in the field, with rather little writing (Dannels, 2005; Dannels, Gaffney, & Martin, 2008).

In Dietetics, interpersonal communication is key during the dietician-client interview, the rather formalized genre that is at the heart of their work (Vrchota, 2011), along with the genre of consultation with the medical doctors. Within both genres, a knowledge of questioning skills, the ability to listen to what is not said, establishing trust, and asserting expertise are important features, which can be taught.

DRR: Clearly there are different oral genres that CID—and WID for that matter—must understand. But you must admit that the research article and its shorter cousin the grant proposal are terribly important genres for scientists and engineers. There writing is dominant, the key to success.

DAV: Yes, and surveys show that working engineers do a great deal of writing on the job, but relatively little writing of research articles. And surveys of professional engineers show that they spend a great deal of their time in meetings, in group work, often in sales, but rather little in preparing and giving formal presentations. Yet most of the CID research in engineering is on presentations. Often professional education efforts privilege the priorities of the academy and so their value in terms of professional preparation is lessened.

DRR: What are the methods most commonly used in CID research?

DAV: Pretty much what you've said. Ethnographic observation, case study. And the data is mostly oral, though we look at documents too (meeting notes, syllabi, etc.). We are looking at different disciplinary cultures. And that provides challenges in our "home culture." When CXC programs were young, there was concern in the

Communication discipline that if faculty in other disciplines taught communication, that the Communication discipline would become obsolete.

DRR: Ah, some Writing people were, and perhaps still are, worried about losing their bread and butter course, too. They worried that WAC would bring about the "abolition" (that's actually the term the critics used) of FYC. But that has never happened that I know of.

DAV: There was also concern that disciplinary faculty who taught Communication would teach skills without theory, thus "watering down" the communication discipline.

DRR: And similarly, there was and is a fear in some quarters in Writing that our expertise would not be valued or would be taught in a reductive and unprincipled way in the disciplines. But that fear is, I think, largely based on an incorrect view that our expertise is a set of techniques to be given to the "natives" in other cultures, rather than the expertise of a consultant, who looks for ways to bring a new perspective, a critical perspective, to what is already going on.

DAV: The broader culture of the academy is very territorial. Maybe that's why writing centers and communication centers are so popular. They are useful without being threatening.

Conclusion

DRR: So I take from our dialogue that there are things we can do together for students in higher education. I'm beginning to see how writing and speaking support learning together. I think that must be happening now in the combined communication and writing centers (Maugh, 2012), where the two traditions are exploring new possibilities. Communication Centers number in the dozens whereas Writing Centers number in the hundreds, maybe thousands by now. I hope an ongoing dialogue between the International Writing Center Association and the National Association of Communication Centers will produce a deeper understanding of WAC/WID/CXC/CID.

One of the things we haven't explored here is how changes in technology are breaking down the barriers between writing and speaking. There are online Communication Centers as well as online Writing Centers, for example, and both written and oral long-distance technology that is being used.

DAV: We've also come across things we can do together for the study and practice of communication in the disciplines and professions. WID and CID are by their very nature working on the boundaries of the disciplines. So maybe we have less turf to protect than we thought and can be more willing to take risks and learn from each other.

Works Cited

Bazerman, C. (2009). Genre and cognitive development: Beyond writing to learn. In C. Bazerman, A. Bonini, & D. Figueiredo (Eds.), *Genre in a Changing World* (pp. 279–294). Fort Collins, CO. : WAC Clearinghouse ; Anderson, SC: Parlor Press.

Bean, J. C. (2011). *Engaging ideas: The professor's guide to integrating writing, critical thinking, and active learning in the classroom.* San Francisco, CA: Jossey-Bass.

Britton, J. N. (1975). *The development of writing abilities* (11-18). London: Macmillan Education.

Cannon, W. W. & Roberts, C.V. (1981, March). *Across the curriculum: The communication skills program at Central College.* Paper presented at the annual meeting of The American Association for Higher Education, Washington, DC.

Cronin, M.W., Grice, G. L., & Palmerton, P.R. (2000). Oral communication across the curriculum: The state of the art after twenty-five years of experience. *Journal of the Association for Communication Administration,* 29, 66-87.

Dannels, D.P. (2005). Performing tribal rituals: A genre analysis of "crits" in design studios. *Communication Education,* 54, 136-160. Doi: 10.1080/03634520500213165

Dannels, D.P., Gaffney, A., & Martin, K. (2008). Beyond Content, deeper than delivery: What critique feedback reveals about communication expectations in design. *International Journal for the Scholarship of teaching and Learning,* 2. Retrieved from http://www.georgiasouthern.edu/ijsotl

Emig, J. (1977). Writing as a mode of learning. *College Composition and Communication,* 28, 122–128.

Gouran, D., & Hirokawa, R. (1983). The role of communication in decision-making groups: A functional perspective. In M. Mander (Ed.). *Communications in transition* (pp. 168-185). New York: Praeger.

Infante, D. (1988). *Arguing constructively.* Prospect Heights, IL: Waveland Press.

Kail, H. (2008). Innovation and repetition: The Brooklyn College Summer Institute in Training Peer Writing Tutors 25 years later. *Writing Center Journal* 28, 43–51.

Klein, P. D. (1999). Reopening inquiry into cognitive processes in writing-to-learn. *Educational Psychology Review,* 11, 203–270.

Latour, B. (2011). Drawing things together. In M. Dodge, R. Kitchin, C. Perkins (Eds.), *The map reader,* (pp. 65–72). Hoboken, NJ: Wiley Blackwell.

Maugh, C. M. (2012). The combined centers approach: How speaking and writing centers can work together. In E. Yook & W. Atkins-Sayre (Eds.), *Communication centers and oral communication programs in higher education: Advantages, challenges, and new directions,* (pp.175-186) Lanham, MD: Lexington Books.

Nystrand, M., Gamoran, A., Kachur, R., & Prendergast, C. (1997). *Opening dialogue.* New York, NY: Teachers College Press. Retrieved from http://www.english.wisc.edu/nystrand/OD1.pdf

Russell, D. R. (2012). «Écrits universitaires/écrits professionnalisants/Écrits professionnels: Est-ce qu'"écrire pour apprendre" est plus qu'un slogan?» [University Writing/Professionalizing Writing/Professional Writing: Is Writing-to-Learn More than a Slogan?] *Pratiques* 155.

Russell, D. R., and Cortes, V. (2012). Academic and scientific texts: the same or different communities? In M. Castello & C. Donahue (Eds.), *University writing: Selves and texts in academic societies,* (pp. 3-17). Bingley, UK: Emerald Publishing.

Shulman, L. (1987). Knowledge and teaching: Foundations of the new reform. *Harvard Educational Review,* 57, 1-22.

Vrchota, D. (2011). Communication in the disciplines: Interpersonal communication in dietetics. *Communication Education,* 60, 210-230.

Yook, E. L., & Atkins-Sayre, W. (Eds.). (2012). *Communication centers and oral communication programs in higher education: Advantages, challenges, and new directions.* Lanham, MD: Lexington Books.

Multidisciplinarity and the Tablet: A Study of Writing Practices

JENNIFER AHERN-DODSON AND DENISE K. COMER

Introduction

> *Profound changes in expressive medium always ask a fundamental question: What does this medium do to us and for us?*
>
> —Richard Lanham, *The Electronic Word*, 1993.

RICHARD LANHAM POSES this question based on the premise that technology is a "rhetorical tool" with the capacity to reshape the values, practices, and possibilities of writing and teaching. Lanham's legacy over the past twenty-plus years has been profound: various iterations of his question have continued to appear as new expressive technologies have emerged and as the "we" to whom Lanham refers has become more broadly imagined: "What does this medium do to us and for us?" As technological media will likely continue to change, "we" (as teachers of writing across disciplines) must continue to ask Lanham's question if we hope to remain engaged with the ways in which lived writing practices persist and change. New technologies may enable changes in writing practices and expectations, and also might reshape the ways in which we write. Whether these changes are positive or negative, welcome or not, they invite us to reexamine our values and practices regarding writing and writing pedagogy, and remind us of the deep role context plays as we enact particular kinds of writing (academic or otherwise) throughout our daily lives.

Perhaps the latest technological medium affecting writing practices is the tablet. Institutions from Seton Hill (Pennsylvania) and Princeton to Oklahoma State and George Fox (Oregon) have been experimenting over the past several years with how to incorporate the tablet, most commonly Apple's iPad, into their pedagogy. This ongoing interest has led some to even suggest that the tablet may be putting pressure on "the future of personal computers" (Hardwick). The possibility that tablets may come to replace personal computers lends an even greater urgency to learning more about how they impact the teaching and learning of writing. Despite (or perhaps due to) the considerable buzz surrounding this emerging technology, hardly any tablet studies have deliberately framed the tablet in the terms by which Lanham's work demands: as a rhetorical tool that shapes writing practices. Using Lanham's frame enables us to pose questions about how tablets impact research, learning, writing and knowledge across and within disciplines. Acknowledging the rhetorical implications of the tablet enables us to think about it not just as a mode of delivery, but within its full range of rhetorical context.

Instead, many studies document what students and faculty generally do with the tablet, and what they like or dislike about the device (Eichenlaub, et al.; "iPad Study"; Bush and Cameron). Most prior tablet research also seems either extra-disciplinary, where data is collected without explicit attention to disciplines (Foresman; Truong), or intra-disciplinary, where data pertains to tablet usage within particular disciplines (Marmarelli and Ringle; Gronke; Schaffhauser). One partial exception to these general trends is a multidisciplinary tablet faculty learning group at Indiana University ("Completed Project"); its findings briefly mention how the tablet intersects with student reading, but do not focus on student writing.[1] Thus, amidst a large and growing body of knowledge on the tablet in higher education, Lanham's question largely remains unanswered: What does the tablet do *to us* or *for us* as writers across disciplines?

To fill this gap, we conducted over the spring and fall of 2011 a multidisciplinary, grant-funded, IRB-approved study at our Research-I institution that explored the following two questions: How does the tablet[2] impact scholarly writing practices across disciplines? How does the tablet impact the teaching of writing across disciplines? Our research extends prior studies about the tablet in higher education by being explicitly multidisciplinary and focused on scholarly writing practices. By integrating multidisciplinary faculty learning groups into our study, we sought to work within the rich tradition of faculty learning groups in Writing Across the Curriculum (WAC) (Carter; Gabelnick, et al.; Walvoord; Anson, *WAC*), particularly as they can be informed by technology (Reiss and Young).

Our study does not emerge from any particular interest in promoting tablets, but instead from a commitment to digital literacy, rhetoric and pedagogy inspired by such scholars as Cynthia Selfe and Kathleen Blake Yancey. They, like Lanham, insist that teachers of writing bear a responsibility to "pay attention to . . . technology" (Selfe, "Technology," 96) as a means of helping students "become the citizen writers of our country, the citizen writers of our world, and the writers of the future" (Yancey

1). Our study also enacts an abiding investment in cultivating multidisciplinary conversations about writing practices and about the teaching of writing, such as those fostered by Susan McLeod and Margot Soven, Art Young, and Toby Fulwiler. Through our study we hoped to create space for faculty and students across disciplines to think explicitly about the relationship between technology and writing. In the following sections we outline our research, discuss how the tablet can impact writing and the teaching of writing, and offer ideas for further research.

The Multidisciplinary Tablet Writing Project

Our university's Center for Instructional Technology awarded us two "Jump-Start Grants" to conduct multidisciplinary tablet projects. These grants included loaner iPad tablets for six faculty members[3] (including us) and up to 80 students in the following spring 2011 and fall 2011 undergraduate writing-intensive courses:

- Environmental Science Seminar: Ethical Challenges in Environmental Conservation (Junior/Senior level; 13 students);
- French 101: Advanced French Composition (two sections, taught by two different instructors; one section had 12 students, one had 11 students);
- Public Policy Seminar: News Writing and Reporting (Junior/Senior level; 16 students); and
- Writing 101: Academic Writing (First-year level; two sections of 12 students each).

Participants included six faculty members, who ranged in rank from adjunct to tenured professor, and 76 undergraduates who ranged in level from first-year through senior. Faculty members were provided with portable keyboards in addition to the iPad tablet; students were not.

We recruited participants by inviting faculty members in humanities, social sciences, and natural sciences with experience teaching writing and an ongoing interest in experimenting with their writing pedagogy. We collected quantitative and qualitative data from faculty and student participants through the following methods: a mid-term attitudinal survey (n=21; see sample questions in Appendix); an end-of term attitudinal survey (n=14; see sample questions in Appendix); student blogs written in one of the Writing 101 sections (n=12); one focus group with faculty participants (n=4); writing-process memos written in one of the Writing 101 sections (n=12); two one-on-one interviews with faculty participants; and teaching journals written by faculty (n=3). We performed qualitative analysis on data through a combination of observer impression, where we examined data and formed impressions, as well as through content analysis, identifying themes and topics that were prominent throughout the data ("Methods").

The tables below show the apps students and faculty in our study used for their scholarly work, and what kinds of writing they did with the tablet.

Table 1: Student Scholarly Apps and Writing

Course	iPad apps	Writing Practices
Environmental Science	Blackboard; Notes; Evernote; iAnnotate; GoodReader; iBooks; Dandelion; Stargazer; Word	reflective journal; calendar for assignments; notes on course texts; notes during class; notes about writing projects; major essays
French	Noterize[4]	respond to peer writing
Public Policy	SoundNote; Notes; Blackboard; Word	notes during a simulated in-class press conference; respond to email; notes during class; notes while reading; news stories; major essays
Writing	Notes; Blackboard; iAnnotate; GoodReader; iBooks; Word; Dropbox; Dragon	notes on course texts; notes during class; notes about writing projects; major essays

Table 2: Faculty Professional and Scholarly Writing

Discipline	Writing Practices
Environmental Science	notes during professional meetings; notes during class
French	respond to student writing; notes on course texts; notes during class
Public Policy	notes during professional meetings; notes during class; email; compose short (1-2 paragraph) drafts
Writing	notes during professional meetings; notes during class; email; compose short (1-2 paragraph) drafts; respond to student writing

How Did the Tablet Impact Scholarly Writing Practices across Disciplines?

According to our research, the tablet seems to increase distinctions between different phases of the writing process, especially between writing notes and in-depth composing. We adopt for this section Keith Hjortshoj's discussion of writing-process phases from *Understanding Writing Blocks*: prewriting, composing, revising, editing and release. In particular, we rely on his distinctions between *prewriting*, "includ[ing] everything the writer does in preparation for composing a text or a portion of a text ... [such as] making preliminary notes and outlines, talking about the subject ... thinking about the task" (25), and *composing*, "the process of generating new sentences and passages that might or might not appear in the finished product—committing words to paper, but not necessarily committing them to the audience" (25).

Writing Notes

One of the most frequently commented-on aspects of the tablet for faculty and student participants was that it improved their practice of writing notes, which falls into Hjortshoj's "prewriting" phase: "It is a convenient and quick way to take notes"; "I don't have to carry my heavy computer around to do writing assignments. In the same vein, I don't have to wait until I am at my computer or in the library to do assignments." While others have also indicated that tablet users appreciate the notes function (Gronke), our multidisciplinary perspective showed that notes are not limited to note-taking during class, but also include generative writing for longer, in-depth writing projects, and note-taking in the field during interviews. That study participants used the tablet for a myriad of different note functions, and commented on this aspect, suggests that using the tablet may have made more visible the distinctions that exist between writing as notes, which most participants found useful on the tablet, and in-depth composing, which most participants found not useful on the tablet (see In-Depth Composing section below).

Notes also emerged as a pedagogical tool through the tablet as different faculty employed notes in various capacities in their classrooms. Four of our faculty participants used iAnnotate for writing notes on student texts, for writing comments on scholarly articles, or by asking students to annotate and comment on their own research project drafts. In these instances, writers combined a scholarly reading practice (annotation) with writing (notes) as part of their work on larger discipline-specific research projects in the courses. Faculty also wrote notes to themselves about aspects of class they planned to follow up on in subsequent classes or adjust in future semesters. Students and faculty wrote to-do lists with notes in order to better organize and plan their scholarly endeavors.[5] As an easy-to-access archive of their thinking about their research through the notes format, writers could see evidence of both writing and thinking development over time. Although a pad of paper could arguably achieve some of the same ends, the tablet seemed to provide participants a way of organizing multiple projects at once by capturing a text electronically to export into a fuller document or combine with another text.

We also discovered that the visibility of notes on the tablet prompted a productive moment of interchange between a faculty member and her students. One of the writing faculty members shared with her students her tablet notes about an on-campus student protest. She then annotated the notes to show students how the notes might be developed into three potential (and different) types of scholarly endeavors: a faculty research project on faculty-student partnerships; a student research topic about how to most effectively promote and publicize a cause; and an idea for a conference proposal on student-activist language. By sharing her notes and delineating three possible writing projects, she demonstrated that when we use notes in this intentional way, they help us remember what research is needed, how we might organize data, and what we might want to rethink or extend. She commented that "this note-taking function [when integrated into a larger discussion of the writing process], enabled students to slow down the research and writing process, to see that good writing takes time and ideas should be allowed to percolate throughout our everyday activities." That so many of our participants commented on writing notes suggests that the tablet encouraged both student and faculty writers to place greater value on notes and fostered greater awareness of their prewriting practices. For many student and faculty writers, the prewriting phase often is undervalued and invisible; students need mentoring throughout the writing process (Bean; Young). However, the readily available and portable notes function of the tablet made students themselves more aware of the value of notes, offering an opportunity to enhance both the practice of prewriting and teaching the critical thinking associated with it.

The ways in which notes emerged differently across each class speak to the complexities of disciplinary context. In the two first-year writing classes, for instance, taught from a humanities perspective, faculty asked students to read scholarly articles in-depth, which included writing annotations. In the public policy course, students were asked to take notes in the field as they reported on various events. In the French courses, students wrote notes on grammar and vocabulary definitions. Rebecca Nowacek suggests that part of what makes interdisciplinarity so challenging, but also so potentially useful, is the concept of the "double bind": "Double binds are those uncomfortable and perhaps inevitable situations in which individuals experience contradictions within or between activity systems (e.g., between the motives and tools within a single activity system or between the motives of two different activity systems) but cannot articulate any meta-awareness of those contradictions" (507). Nowacek's point is that these double binds emerge because of what David Russell has identified as a systemic problem with disciplinary divisions: faculty often learn how to write from within their particular disciplines and are therefore underprepared in considering how their own discipline's activity systems are unique and contextualized.[6]

For faculty participants in our study, the tablet learning community created the opportunity for a multidisciplinary conversation about what we expect in student writing and about how we teach writing; this process and the ensuing conversations tapped into these double binds and offered faculty the opportunity to enact Nowacek's "meta-awareness of those contradictions." We contend that not only should faculty in learning communities engage in these kinds of multidisciplinary meta-discussions about their writing practices and the implications of "double-binds," but students should be invited to participate as well—both in faculty-student learning communities and within individual courses. By participating in such a group, faculty and students can deepen their consideration of writing practices—and beliefs about how writing should happen—potentially opening up additional avenues for cross-disciplinary dialogue beyond the tablet study.

In-Depth Composing

Despite the tablet's success with writing notes, most participants indicated that the tablet was difficult or counterproductive for in-depth composing, and instead chose their laptops for "the paper" or "the journal article." Comments about in-depth composing generally fell into three categories: 1) difficulty with the touchscreen ("Writing with our fingers and typing on the iPad] were clumsier than simply writing with a pen on paper would have been"); 2) frustration with word-processing functions ("local word processing applications . . . completely inadequate"); and 3) difficulty changing writing practices ("If I can't even remember my iTunes account, how am I going to take time to really understand the mechanisms for creating, saving, transferring files? I loved the iPad for notes because it was easier to organize my notes, file, keep track of my ideas, and I didn't lose random pieces of paper. But writing on it felt like too big of a change to be worth the learning curve.").

Taken together, these three categories of dissatisfaction suggest that the dislike of in-depth composing on the tablet, for some writers, may be connected primarily with a lack of familiarity and experience with touch-screen typing. Writing practices often are replete with personal idiosyncrasies, and writers might be disinclined to use a new technology for in-depth composing if they have already found mechanisms that work well for them, as would likely be the case for a faculty member. Indeed, while our study's faculty participants were willing to experiment with the tablet in their reading practices and in their *teaching* of writing, they were not as willing to experiment with the tablet for their own writing practices. As one faculty member commented,

> Although I often look for ways to enhance and strengthen my personal writing practices, I am reluctant to look for ways of deeply reconceiving how I write because I'd rather devote energy to the ideas and the projects I want to create. While I wish I could find ways of publishing even more, it felt like it would be a step back to learn to write on the iPad.... Some people of an earlier generation of scholars than me still write by hand because the way they think is connected to the medium through which they write. They may take advantage of certain new technologies, but not to change how they write.

Others have noted resistance and dissatisfaction with in-depth composing on the tablet (Kolowich; Gronke). Such findings make the tablet somewhat unique among other digital platforms, which studies have shown generally facilitate significant advantages to in-depth composing (Pennington; Hult; Reiss and Young). The advantages we now see with in-depth composing on most digital platforms, however, were not universally apparent when computers first emerged. Several early studies suggested that computers did not encourage critical revision (Hawisher, "The Effects") or caused underperformance (Dean). The tablet might be facing a similar trajectory as touch-screen technology is becoming more ubiquitous with infrastructures, phones and tablets; however, for the time being, the tablet seems to have a negative effect on in-depth composing for most students and faculty because of limited word-processing functionality such as composing for long periods of time, facility with the process of moving from thought to text, and moving and deleting text.

Although the tablet enables (and even fosters with deliberate attention in teaching) pre-writing as well as the concept that writing can happen in short bursts of time, we wonder at what cost. Do we expect students (and faculty) to have both a tablet and a laptop to enhance both pre-writing and in-depth composing practices? How likely is it for academic writers to see using two devices as enhancing their writing process, rather than hindering or complicating it?

How Did the Tablet Impact the Teaching of Writing across Disciplines?

Over twenty years ago, Gail Hawisher and Cynthia Selfe argued for deliberateness when integrating technology into the classroom: "All too frequently . . . writing instructors incorporate computers into their classes without the necessary scrutiny and careful planning that the use of any technology requires" ("Rhetoric" 35). Moreover, Janet Eldred argues that the effective use of technology requires linking it to the pedagogical goals of the course.[7] Such cautions are especially important with the tablet, since it runs the risk of being perceived as redundant technology, or it might not even be officially incorporated in the classroom but brought into use by students outside of class. Faculty, therefore, might not perceive a need for "careful planning." The tablet, though, offers some markedly different features than laptops, and includes an ever growing and shifting range of apps. This complex realm of possibilities contrasts some of our expectations about technology. As Anson claims, "we see [technological advances] as a promise to simplify our lives and streamline our work" ("Distant Voices" 53). These concerns about simplification and about how well the tablet fits within the larger aims of a course emerged in our study as faculty reported that the tablet shaped their course design and pedagogy in the following two ways: writing assignments and responding to student writing.

Writing Assignments

Several faculty participants created new assignments specifically geared toward the tablet, most notably Environmental Science and Public Policy.[8]

1. *Environmental Science.* This faculty member viewed the tablet's increased portability and the environmentally related apps as an opportunity to encourage students to forge a closer relationship with the environment: "I had visions of students composing essays while sitting under an oak in [the forest], blogging about the latest environmental news from the Marketplace, and finding new cool apps that help us to live green!" To facilitate such engagement, she developed the following two tablet-specific writing assignments:
   - record experiences in nature through a tablet journal; and
   - record and annotate an interview about the environment with a community member.

   Despite student interest in these endeavors, though, her students expressed concern about the tablet's use of resources and energy: "Saved some paper . . . but not enough to justify manufacture/cost of the device." The faculty member began to question the inclusion of the tablet in her course: "In a class where I was asking students to think about the use of resources, I then saw that they were using iPads in addition to, rather than instead of, their laptops. It seemed to increase resource use rather than decrease it." She eventually came to see journaling on a tablet as ironic within the context of an Environmental Science course:

   > [The dandelion app] presents an image of a dandelion, with its fluffy, white seeds almost sparkling on the screen. You blow on the screen and—poof—the seeds disperse out into the electronic atmosphere. If my students are wasting time making wishes on electronic dandelions, then clearly we have a problem. Our challenge is to become more

connected to nature, to better understand our role as stewards and our impacts as citizens.

Because this teacher implicitly valued students connecting to nature in meaningful ways and appreciating their responsibilities as "stewards" and "citizens" of the natural world, her choice to integrate the tablet into her course was based on the tablet's potential to help students with these aspirations. Her growing hesitations over the tablet's inefficacy for teaching writing were based predominantly on this discipline-specific value. Although students were physically *in* nature, their focus was *on* the screen. In fact, they didn't need to sit among the trees to write their journal entries at all. Despite the tablet's portability, then, it interfered with, rather than enhanced, students' meaningful connections with nature.

2. *Public Policy.* Whereas the tablet seemed to the Environmental Science instructor to be counterproductive to some of the primary learning outcomes of her class, it had an affinity toward the broader learning objectives of the News Writing and Reporting seminar. This faculty member also shaped assignments based on the tablet, and saw the device as a way of facilitating his larger endeavor of introducing students to several crucial features of contemporary journalism: the need to have access to large and varying kinds of information in the field and the ability to deliver news stories quickly from the field. He designed the following writing assignments specifically using the tablet:
   - record weekly interviews around the campus and community;
   - record an in-class mock press conference; and
   - write news stories quickly and on deadline, often from the field.

This faculty member found the tablet of great potential use within journalism: "The news gathering industry is in transition mode as exemplified by concepts such as 'backpack journalism,' in which one person takes everything s/he needs to cover a story in a variety of media formats." For News Writing and Reporting, then, it seems that the tablet was able to forward disciplinary aims by helping facilitate students' learning of real-world journalism.

Together, these experiences suggest that integrating the tablet may help faculty rethink writing assignments, but it also reinforces the importance of considering how a given technology intersects with the larger goals, discourse, activities, and aspirations of particular faculty and disciplines.

Responding to Student Writing

There is much literature on responding to student writing, and our study has been most influenced by research related to faculty responding styles (Straub and Lunsford; Anson, "Response Styles"), response and its relationship to writer development (Sommers; Hyland and Hyland) and the facilitative role of technology in response to student writing (Comer and Hammer; Lynne; Reiss and Young; Nortcliffe and Middleton).

We found that faculty used the tablets to respond to student writing in dramatically different ways. The first-year writing faculty chose not to use the tablet for responding to student writing. They indicated that they were reluctant to take the time to experiment with a new responding technology, and they were fairly content with their current response strategies and tools. The environmental science faculty member enjoyed the portability of the tablet because it provided a wider range of occasions for her to respond to student writing: "I liked that the iPad enabled me to take my work with me more easily. I could even respond to students' writing while I was at the playground with my children." The tablet, then, afforded her more cohesion between her professional and personal activities. For her, responding to student writing while "in nature" and with her children positively influenced her attitude toward response (she was a happier responder). Still, while she liked being able to read student papers at the playground, she much preferred commenting by hand and did not make much use of the tablet for responding.

The French teachers, however, both keenly interested in the tablet's potential to facilitate high-quality feedback efficiently, used the tablet much more extensively for responding to student writing. They used the Noterize app to provide color-coded and audio responses to student writing in one PDF file. Their students responded with enthusiasm: "It . . . enhanced the experience of receiving comments from my prof."; "having the ipad . . . made things more efficient (like receiving and storing my professor's comments)"; "I really like hearing the faculty feedback. Mostly because I would hear my prof musing about [the paper] . . . I also liked hearing the feedback because it was more personal and more like discussing it with [her]." One French faculty member indicated that she paid greater attention to her commenting because of the tablet and could focus both on grammar/text 'corrections' and the 'writing/writers.' She felt she was able to move beyond "corrective feedback" to become a more engaged reader of student writing (Vyatkina). Her interest in the tablet as a teaching and responding tool, her ongoing informal assessment of the way it shaped her teaching throughout the semester (teaching journal) and her participation in the research project all prompted a more critical analysis of her responding style and its influence on students.[9] Although certainly there are other options for audio or even video response to student writing,[10] this faculty member found the tablet's apps and portability worked for her and enhanced the quality of her response and her own engagement with student writing. She commented, "Before this semester I was dreading teaching writing again," and she felt that students were often just "going through the motions" of revision after reviewing her comments on drafts. She was not engaged; they were not engaged. After experimenting with the tablet and her own responding style, she discovered a renewed commitment to teaching writing and, in fact, looked forward to teaching the course again.

The public policy faculty member used the tablet to read lower-stakes student writing and write brief comments, but chose not to use the tablet for more in-depth responses because he prefers instead to introduce students to journalistic red-pen editing and correction. He found the tablet a barrier to this mode of commentary. Although he could have explored virtual red-pen commenting options, the literal red-pen response is a deeply-held responding practice for him and one that he finds crucially embedded in his discipline.

Overall, faculty made decisions about using the tablet for responding based on 1) their perceived level of need to improve or experiment with responding strategies; 2) their perceived level of time, energy and availability for adjusting responding strategies; and 3) their perceptions about discipline-specific expectations and practices for responding to student writing. Thus, while the tablet yielded positive results for responding to student writing in the L2 courses (whose faculty were eager to experiment with responding strategies, despite the learning curve), students and faculty in the other classes seemed not to find value in the tablet for response to student writing because they already had strategies that worked, simply were not interested in developing a new strategy or felt that it departed from disciplinary conventions. These findings suggest to us that point of need, faculty investment and disciplinary context are factors that play a greater role in response than does the tablet itself.

Further Research

We see two critical areas for additional research:

1. *Student Writing.* Continued research is needed on the ways the tablet may affect scholarly reading and writing practices and the teaching of writing. Given our data from the French courses, we call specifically for more research on faculty responses to student writing and peer-response practices with the tablet or other e-reading devices: Is the tablet any different from other audio or video tools responders might use? How might the tablet influence the various faculty and student responding roles and purposes? Toward what ends?

2. *Power, Privilege, and the Tablet.* The question of access, familiarity, power and privilege with tablets will, we believe, affect literacy practices differently across individuals and institutional contexts. Although our study was conducted at a private, Research-I institution with strong support for technology grants, many of our students' experiences reveal what David Bolt and Ray Crawford (and others) term the "digital divide."[11] We call for more research into how tablets intersect with assumptions about students' access to technology and its use in scholarly contexts.[12] How might tablets reduce or expand the divide between students who do or do not have access to technology? Given the portability and convenience of tablets, will they provide an educational advantage or disadvantage to those who have them?

Conclusion and Implications: Did the Tablet Improve Student Writing?

Our research certainly indicated that the tablet did things *to us* and *for us* as writers and teachers of writing, but—and here is the implied significance of Lanham's question—to what end? The tablet works best when used for the following occasions: prewriting and making research and writing processes visible for students. We know the tablet did not work well for in-depth composing. Encouraging teachers of writing to be more innovative in assignment creation and response strategies and facilitating interdisciplinary conversations, unhinging us from our double binds, should have a positive effect on student writing by helping students understand the significance of context, audience and purpose within and across disciplines. However, when we asked the faculty participants whether student writing improved with the integration of the iPad tablet in their courses, only one of the six (a French faculty member) indicated that she thought it probably did; the other five were unsure. The tablet runs the risk of seeming to users that it is just a more portable, lighter version of a computer. Our data, however, reveal limitations with in-depth composing on a tablet and thus demonstrate that the tablet is not just a more portable, lighter computer. Without deliberate attention to the tablet as a unique technology, we face a possible risk of reinforcing, or abiding by, or not noticing, ineffective writing practices. Without an explicit discussion about writing practices and conditions, students who are encouraged to—or choose to of their own volition—use the tablet for scholarly writing may in fact end up adapting their writing practices to meet the limited functionality of the device. We are concerned that the material conditions of writing on the tablet might dictate practice.

Our own personal experiences with the tablet reflect in some ways this seduction. As researchers who not only were studying faculty and student use of the tablet, but also enthusiastically experimenting with tablets ourselves (each of us received an iPad for two semesters as part of our research grants), we were interested in identifying ways this device might transform the teaching of writing or the ways that we understand those practices. Any limitations we identified initially we attributed to user error or to lack of experience, rather than limitations in the device itself. During the academic year, however, our enthusiasm for the tablet diminished. We found it practical for some professional purposes (taking notes during meetings, skimming various kinds of texts, writing quick emails, pre-writing, etc.), but we found ourselves using it less and less for our own scholarly and work-related writing. This gradual shift in practice, though, may have occurred in part because we are more experienced writers, and we work to be aware of our writing practices. Students, many of whom are presumably less experienced as writers, may not be as inclined to embrace the agency demanded by the tablet and could instead let the device shape and dictate their writing practices, perhaps in ways that may challenge longstanding values in academia: namely, the importance of in-depth, sustained composing.

Addressing this possibility places heightened emphasis on what Dennis Baron has argued—that we should continue to question and notice our priorities with technology and literacy practices:

> But maybe the most significant thing that we can learn from putting today's digital reading and writing in the context of five thousand years of literacy history, using past results to predict future performance, is that the digitized text permeating our lives today is the next stage, not the last stage, in the saga of human communication, and that it's impossible to tell from what we're doing now exactly where it is that we will be going with our words tomorrow. (246)

Baron's point, like Lanham's before him, and like others before and since, is that the most meaningful way we can work with technologies such as the tablet is to pay attention to and reflect on the ways in which they shape writing practices. We discovered that the tablet reshaped for some students and faculty several key writing practices, such as writing notes. Our multidisciplinary tablet faculty-learning group enabled faculty to design writing courses that were more deliberate and innovative; it helped make those courses more engaging for students in a variety of ways. We found that interdisciplinary conversations about writing shifted with the introduction of the tablet.

While other scholars have made the point that technologies should be deployed with deliberate attention, we want to underscore that the tablet may seem like it is not necessarily a new technology. To some, the tablet has the appearance of merely being a smaller, more portable computer that uses apps instead of a hard drive. This may make these individuals unlikely to differentiate the tablet from a laptop. As such, some faculty might not see the need to spend time deliberately integrating the tablet into a classroom. Unlike medium-specific writing occasions, where teachers might ask students to design a webpage or use Twitter, students might on their own be using tablets for all sorts of writing assignments without even finding it relevant to communicate that choice to the teacher. However, the tablet shapes writing practices differently than does a computer. Thus, this lure of similarity between computers and tablets creates even more urgency for teachers and students across disciplines to reflect on the contexts for writing, to be aware of how material conditions shape writing, and to make deliberate choices about which kinds of technologies they will use for different writing performances. In this way, students and faculty alike will be able to have more control over what the tablet does to us and for us as writers across disciplines.

Acknowledgments

Support for this research—and for the use of iPad tablets in these classes—was given by the Center for Instructional Technology at Duke University. We'd like to thank all the faculty and students who participated in our study. We'd also like to thank Monique Dufour, Andrea Novicki, participants in the August 2012 Postdoctoral Summer Seminar in Teaching Writing for their feedback on early drafts of this article, and the editor and reviewers of *WAC Journal* for providing feedback throughout the revision process.

Notes

1. Their final report briefly notes, "[T]he iPad also suggests utility as a reading device for electronic textbooks (as well as a method of reviewing, creating, and responding to other instructional material and media)" ("Completed Project").

2. Our study focused on iPad tablets specifically, but we use the more general term *tablet* throughout the essay.

3. The French faculty members were awarded loaner iPads for their courses as a separate "Jump Start" grant but were included in this research study.

4. Noterize has since been purchased by Nuance.

5. These kinds of notes reflect what Eichenlaub, et al., term, "Organizing academic workflows with the iPads": "Project iPad provided participants with the opportunity to develop new approaches for time management and organization in their personal and academic lives" (18).

6. See also Carter, "Ways of Knowing, Doing, and Writing in the Disciplines."

7. We have found the work of Cynthia Selfe (Multimodal), Wayne Jacobson and Donald Wulff, Deborah Hatch and Kimberly Emmons, and Erping Zhu and Matthew Kaplan useful in

making the case with faculty across the disciplines for an intentional inclusion of the tablet and alignment with course and disciplinary learning goals.

8. The other faculty modified existing assignments.

9. See also Ahern-Dodson and Reisinger, "Moving beyond Corrective Feedback to Engage Students as Writers and Faculty as Readers." (MS in Preparation)

10. Camtasia and Jing, for instance, provide audio and video feedback options. For research on the impact of audio and video feedback, see Reynolds and Russell; and Jones, Georghiades, and Gunson.

11. Several student participants expressed a disinclination to purchase "expensive" apps; some students indicated familiarity with the iPad tablet because one of their family members already had one, and one student planned on asking her parents for one as a Christmas gift. Meanwhile, other students indicated feeling newly equipped to navigate academia with a portable, continual connectivity that they previously did not have through phones, much less a tablet.

12. See Elmer-DeWitt and "iPad Ownership" for demographics of iPad ownership; Steven J. Vaughan-Nichols on the iPad's impact on K-12 systems; Pillar on the "technological underclass" (218); Selfe and Selfe on "domination and colonialism associated with computer use" (66); and Bush and Cameron on ADA compliance.

Works Cited

Ahern-Dodson, Jennifer, and Deb Reisinger. "Moving Beyond Corrective Feedback to Engage Students as Writers and Faculty as Readers." Unpublished manuscript. 2012.

Anson, Chris M. "Distant Voices: Teaching and Writing in a Culture of Technology." Sidler, Morris, and Smith 46-63. Print.

— "Response Styles and Ways of Knowing." *Writing and Response: Theory, Practice, and Research*. Ed. Chris M. Anson. Urbana: National Council of Teachers of English, 1989. 332-66. Print.

— *The WAC Casebook: Scenes for Faculty Reflection and Program Development*. New York: Oxford UP, 2002. Print.

Baron, Dennis. *A Better Pencil: Readers, Writers, and the Digital Revolution*. New York: Oxford UP, 2009. Print.

Bean, John. *Engaging Ideas: The Professor's Guide to Integrating Writing, Critical Thinking, and Active Learning in the Classroom*. San Francisco: Jossey-Bass, 2001. Print.

Bolt, David, and Ray Crawford. *Digital Divide: Computers and Our Children's Future*. New York: TV Books, 2000. Print.

Bush, Michael H., and Andrea H. Cameron. "Digital Course Materials: A Case Study of the Apple iPad in the Academic Environment." PhD diss. Pepperdine University, 2011. ProQuest. Web. 2 Apr. 2012.

Caldwell, Elizabeth Ann, and Mary Deane Sorcinelli. "The Role of Faculty Development Programs in Helping Teachers to Improve Student Learning through Writing." *Writing to Learn: Strategies for Assigning and Responding to Writing across the Disciplines. New Directions for Teaching and Learning* 69. Ed. Mary Deane Sorcinelli and Peter Elbow. San Francisco: Jossey-Bass, 1997. 141-49. Print.

Carter, Michael. "Ways of Knowing, Doing, and Writing in the Disciplines." *College Composition and Communication* 58 (2007): 385-418. Web. 29 May 2012.

Comer, Denise, and Brad Hammer. "Surveying the Efficacy of Digital Response: Pedagogical Imperatives, Faculty Approaches, and Student Feedback." *Writing and the iGeneration. Composition in the Computer-Mediated Classroom.* Ed. Terry Carter and Maria Clayton. Southlake: Fountainhead P, 2008. 99-120. Print.

"Completed Project: iPad Faculty Learning Communities: Exploring Innovative Teaching and Learning with the Apple iPad." *University Information Technology Services.* Indiana University, 1 May 2012. Web. 31 May 2012.

Dean, Robert L. "Cognitive, Pedagogic, and Financial Implications of Word Processing in a Freshman English Program: A Report on Two Years of a Longitudinal Study." 26th Annual Forum of the Association for Institutional Research. Orlando, FL. June 1986. Conference Presentation. *ERIC.* Web. 1 June 2012.

Eichenlaub, Naomi, Laine Gabel, Dan Jakubek, Graham McCarthy, and Weina Wang. "Project iPad: Investigating Tablet Integration in Learning and Libraries at Ryerson University." *Computers in Libraries* 31.7 (2011): 17-21. ProQuest. Web. 26 May 2012.

Elbow, Peter. "High Stakes and Low Stakes in Assigning and Responding to Writing." *Writing to Learn: Strategies for Assigning and Responding to Writing across the Disciplines. New Directions for Teaching and Learning* 69. Ed. Mary Deane Sorcinelli and Peter Elbow. San Francisco: Jossey-Bass, 1997. 5-13. Print.

Eldred, Janet M. "Pedagogy in the Computer-networked Classroom." Sidler, Morris, and Smith 239-250. Print.

Elmer-DeWitt, Philip. "Apple's New iPad: The Analysts Weigh In." *CNN Money.* CNN, 8 Mar. 2012. Web. 23 May 2012.

Foresman, Chris. "Apple's iPad Goes to College This Fall." *CNN Tech.* CNN, 27 July 2010. Web. 18 May 2012.

Gabelnick, Faith, et al., eds. *Learning Communities: Creating Connections among Students, Faculty, and Disciplines. New Directions for Teaching and Learning* 41. San Francisco: Jossey-Bass, 1990. Print.

Gronke, Paul. "Somewhere in the Middle. A Comment on Steve Kolowich's 'Apple of Their Eye?'" *Inside Higher Ed.* Inside Higher Ed, 22 Dec. 2010. Web. 23 May 2012.

Hardwick, Joshua. "Apple iPad Holds 82 Percent Tablet PC Market Share in United States." *Tablet PC News & Reviews.* Tablet PC Lab, 7 May 2011. Web. 23 May 2012.

Hatch, Deborah, and Kimberly Emmons. "Aligning through Writing." *Aligning for Learning: Strategies for Teaching Effectiveness.* Ed. Donald Wulff. Boston: Anker, 2005. 162-76. Print.

Hawisher, Gail E. "The Effects of Word Processing on the Revision Strategies of College Freshmen." *Research in the Teaching of English* 21.2 (1987): 145-59. JSTOR. Web. 1 June 2012.

Hawisher, Gail E., and Cynthia L. Selfe. "The Rhetoric of Technology and the Electronic Writing Class." Sidler, Morris, and Smith 35-45. Print.

Hjortshoj, Keith. *Understanding Writing Blocks*. New York: Oxford UP, 2001. Print.

Hult, Christine A. "The Computer and the Inexperienced Writer." Sidler, Morris, and Smith 326-332. Print.

Hyland, Fiona, and Ken Hyland. "Sugaring the Pill: Praise and Criticism in Written Feedback." *Journal of Second Language Writing* 10 (2001): 185-212. Science Direct. Web. 1 June 2012.

"iPad Ownership Grows Among all US Income Segments." *comScore Data Mine*. comScore, Inc., 7 Mar. 2012. Web. 23 May 2012.

"iPad Study Released by Oklahoma State University." *Business Wire*. Business Wire, 3 May 2011. Web. 23 May 2012.

Jacobson, Wayne and Donald Wulff. "Designing for Alignment." *Aligning for Learning: Strategies for Teaching Effectiveness*. Ed. Donald Wulff. Boston: Anker, 2005. 35-50. Print.

Jones, Nigel, Panicos Georghiades, and John Gunson. "Student Feedback Via Screen Capture Digital Video: Stimulating Student's Modified Action." *Higher Education*. 9 Mar 2012. 1-15. Web. 2 Aug 2012.

Kolowich, Steve. "Apple of Their Eye?" *Inside Higher Ed*. Inside Higher Ed, 22 Dec. 2010. Web. 25 May 2012.

Lanham, Richard. *The Electronic Word: Democracy, Technology, and the Arts*. Chicago: U of Chicago P, 1993. Print.

Lynne, Patricia. "Seeing Rainbows: Using Color-Coding to Guide Revision." *Writing and the iGeneration. Composition in the Computer-Mediated Classroom*. Ed. Terry Carter and Maria Clayton. Southlake: Fountainhead P, 2008. 141-160. Print.

Marmarelli, Trina, and Martin Ringle. "The Reed College iPad Study. Summary of Faculty Evaluation Reports." Portland: Reed College. April 2011. *Reed College*. Web. 18 May 2012.

McLeod, Susan, ed. *Strengthening Programs for Writing across the Curriculum*. San Francisco: Jossey-Bass, 1988. Print.

McLeod, Susan, Eric Miraglia, Margot Soven, and Christopher Thaiss, eds. *WAC for the New Millenium*. Urbana: NCTE, 2001. Print.

McLeod, Susan, and Margot Soven. *Writing across the Curriculum: A Guide to Developing Programs*. Newbury Park: Sage, 1992. Print.

"Methods of Qualitative Data Analysis." *Qualitative Data Analysis*. Qualitative Data Analysis, 2010. Web. 25 July 2013.

Nortcliffe, Anne, and Andrew Middleton. *Audio Feedback for the iPod Generation*. International Conference on Engineering Education. Coimbra, Portugal. Conference Presentation. Sept. 2007. Web. 30 May 2012.

Nowacek, Rebecca S. "Why Is Being Interdisciplinary So Very Hard to Do?" *College Composition and Communication* 60.3 (2009): 493–516. Print.

Pennington, Martha C. "The Impact of the Computer in Second Language Writing." Sidler, Morris, and Smith 404-424. Print.

Pillar, Charles. "Separate Realities: The Creation of the Technological Underclass in America's Public Schools." *MacWorld* 9.9 (1992): 218-230. ProQuest. Web. 22 May 2012.

Reiss, Donna, Dickie Selfe, and Art Young. *Electronic Communication across the Curriculum*. Urbana, IL: NCTE, 1998. Print.

—. and Art Young. "WAC Wired: Electronic Communication across the Curriculum." Sidler, Morris, and Smith 425-447. Print.

Reynolds, Julie, and Vicki Russell. "Can You Hear Us Now? A Comparison of Peer Review Quality When Students Give Audio Versus Written Feedback." *The WAC Journal* 19 (2008): 29-44. Print.

Russell, David. *Writing in the Academic Disciplines, 1870-1990: A Curricular History*. Carbondale, IL: Southern Illinois UP, 1991. Print.

Schaffhauser, Dian. "Duke U Trying Out iPads for Field Research." *Campus Technology*. Media Inc.13 July 2010. Web. 28 May 2012.

— "iPad Pilot Launches in Texas University MBA Program." *Campus Technology*. Media Inc., 8 Sept. 2010. Web. 28 May 2012.

Selfe, Cynthia, ed. *Multimodal Composition: Resources for Teachers*. Cresskill, NJ: Hampton, 2007. Print.

—. "Technology and Literacy: A Story about the Perils of Not Paying Attention." Sidler, Morris, and Smith 93-115. Print.

Selfe, Cynthia, and Richard J. Selfe, Jr. "The Politics of the Interface: Power and Its Exercise in Electronic Contact Zones." Sidler, Morris, and Smith 64-85. Print.

Sidler, Michelle, Richard Morris, and Elizabeth Overman Smith, eds. *Computers in the Composition Classroom. A Critical Sourcebook*. Boston: Bedford/St. Martin's, 2008. Print.

Sommers, Nancy. "Across the Drafts." *College Composition and Communication* 58.2 (2006): 248-257. JSTOR. Web. 1 June 2012.

Straub, Richard. "Students' Reactions to Teacher Comments: An Exploratory Study. *Research in the Teaching of English* 31 (1997): 91-119. JSTOR. Web. 1 June 2012.

Straub, Richard, and Ronald F. Lunsford. *12 Readers Reading: Responding to College Student Writing*. Cresskill, NJ: Hampton, 1995. Print.

Truong, Kelly. "More Universities Announce iPad Experiments." *Wired Campus*. The Chronicle of Higher Education, 20 July 2010. Web. 22 May 2012.

Vaughan-Nichols, Steven J. "The Poor Get Poorer and the Rich Get Richer with Apple's iPad-Based Textbooks." *ZDNet*. CBS Interactive, 22 Jan. 2012. Web. 20 May 2012.

Vyatkina, Nina. "Writing Instruction and Policies for Written Corrective Feedback in the Basic Language." *L2 Journal* 3.1 (2011): 63-92. *eScholarship*. Web. 1 June 2012.

Walvoord, Barbara. "The Future of WAC." *College English* 58 (1996): 58-79. Print.

Yancey, Kathleen Blake. "*Writing in the 21st Century. A Report from the NCTE.*" Urbana: National Council of Teachers of English, 2009. Report. NCTE. Web. 31 May 2012.

Young, Art. *Teaching Writing across the Curriculum.* Upper Saddle River: Prentice Hall, 1999. Print.

Young, Art, and Toby Fulwiler. *Writing across the Disciplines.* Research into Practice. Upper Montclair: Boynton/Cook, 1986. Print.

Zhu, Erping, and Matthew Kaplan. "Technology and Teaching." *McKeachie's Teaching Tips.* Ed. Marilla Svinicki and Wilbert McKeachie. 13th ed. Belmont: Wadsworth, 2011. 235-66. Print.

Appendix

Sample Questions from Mid-Term and End-of-Term Attitudinal Surveys

- Please list some adjectives or phrases describing your experience using the iPad to read course texts.
- What do you like about using the iPad for scholarly reading?
- What do you dislike about using the iPad for your scholarly reading?
- Do you have any other comments about your experience using the iPad for scholarly reading?
- Have you used the iPad for scholarly writing this semester?
- List some adjectives or phrases describing your experience using the iPad for scholarly writing.
- What do you like about using the iPad for scholarly writing?
- What do you dislike about using the iPad for your scholarly writing?
- Do you have any other comments regarding your use of the iPad for scholarly writing?

Committed to WAC: Christopher Thaiss

INTERVIEWED BY CAROL RUTZ

CHRISTOPHER "CHRIS" THAISS has served the writing across the curriculum (WAC) cause for many years in multiple ways. Currently, he is the Clark Kerr Presidential Chair and Professor in the University Writing Program at the University of California at Davis, splitting that appointment with the directorship of the UC Davis Center for Excellence in Teaching and Learning. During this interview, Chris reviews his personal educational and scholarly history, which I will not repeat here.

Widely appreciated for his scholarship, Chris has personified WAC pedagogy, theory, and ideals through his teaching, research, and publication. With talented co-authors (all of whom are credited as part of this interview), he has been an agent of discovery and documentation. Without Chris Thaiss, the WAC Mapping Project would not exist, nor would the follow-up study by his co-author, Tara Porter, now underway. Without Chris Thaiss, his pedagogical instincts, his collaborative energy, and his eloquence, the WAC world would be a less defined, under-theorized intellectual place. Fortunately, Chris remains engaged in WAC work for the duration—may his commitment never flag.

If this interview seems longer than some others published in *The WAC Journal* in recent years, the reason lies in an impressive range of topics, problems, and ideas that Chris brings to my questions. Among the themes developed: scholarship and pedagogy as mutually informing; collaboration as a positive professional experience; WAC legacy of exploration and innovation (an evocation of the spirit of the Renaissance); international connections for WAC programs and scholarship; healthy prospects for WAC; concern about standardized assessments; surprise at the limitations of much WAC research; and possible connections with MOOCs. All of these goodies were collected through correspondence and a lengthy interview over lunch at the 2013 convention of the Conference on College Composition and Communication (CCCC or Cs) in Las Vegas.

Throughout, Chris's enthusiasm for learning as well as his excitement about future possibilities offers a portrait of a senior WAC scholar who is just getting started. That paradox will make sense to readers as you explore with me a tiny slice of Chris Thaiss' world. Read on.

Carol Rutz: Few scholars are as personally identified with WAC as you are, yet you are of a generation that came to writing studies and WAC more specifically through a literature route. What can you tell *The WAC Journal* readers about your professional journey?

Chris Thaiss: I like that "of a generation." I know what that means! Well, yes, there were no rhet/comp programs when I came through grad school (Northwestern, 1975), where I concentrated in Renaissance (also known as Early Modern) literature in England. But my interest in that literary period was not antiquarian: what I admired about the Elizabethans and their Continental counterparts was their sense of adventure and of a break with the medieval past, manifest in the voyages of discovery, the revival of the Greek and Roman classics, the new science, and the explosion of literature and transnational communication catalyzed by the spread of printing. I was totally mesmerized at the time by the whole Elizabethan myth. I didn't realize at the time that my reading classical and Renaissance rhetoric would have so much relevance to what I would wind up doing with my life.

I had the good fortune at Northwestern to meet Wallace Douglas. Wally had a joint appointment in English and Education, and he inspired me with his love of teaching. I also came just at the time that Northwestern launched a training course for teaching assistants (TAs), and so I began reading Wilbert McKeachie and other eloquent advocates for undergraduate teaching. Then, when I began teaching as an adjunct in Virginia at George Mason University and Northern Virginia Community College in 1975, I thoroughly enjoyed teaching composition and became the first tutor in the new GMU writing lab.

The founder of that tutorial effort was GMU faculty member Don Gallehr, who two years later would found the Northern Virginia Writing Project, and who would ask me to "co-direct" (really, be an assistant). It's ironic that in 1976 I was hired as an assistant professor, to teach Renaissance courses (and intro comp and lit), because once the Writing Project got going in 1978, I was pretty quickly transformed into this "new" thing called a compositionist. (I don't think we actually used that term until quite a bit later.) By 1979, I had taken over as director of comp and director of the writing lab (renamed the writing center in the early 80s)—*and* coordinator of this cool thing called "writing across the curriculum." All this in three years, while I was still an assistant professor. Such a thing was possible at GMU in those days, when it was a comparatively small and new place, and an assistant professor's having these kinds of administrative adventures was not a hindrance to getting tenure, but, at least in my case, a help.

It's important to keep in mind that I have never seen a disjunction between my Renaissance studies and my teaching/administration of writing. Sure, the rhetorical continuum is one obvious link, but more profound for me is the link through experimental "let's try this new thing" culture heroes like Shakespeare, Erasmus, and Bacon. Since I come from immigrant farmers and craftspeople, I'm always attracted to stories of clever "by your bootstraps" types who like to try new stuff and don't mind organizing things. I guess that's one reason why I didn't have much trouble uprooting from Virginia in 2006, after 30 years, to go West to the University of California-Davis, which is a similar place in its entrepreneurial ways and has taken me back to my family's farming roots.

It's that same perspective on life that drew me to the teaching of writing and lured me away from literary history. It was easier for me to see how a writing class could help striving young persons achieve their goals, whatever those might be. After all, writing fits with any dream of moving forward. I enjoyed the lit classes I taught, but I always had the feeling that I was trying to sell the love and value of literature to students. Students would have to accommodate themselves to the texts, whereas writing can accommodate almost any self, because it is so flexible and variously useful.

CR: What a stunning combination of scholarly and pedagogical passions. Can you categorize the programs and projects that have most engaged you as a teacher and scholar? For example, your work with Terry Myers Zawacki at George Mason University had as much to do with faculty as graduate or undergraduate students. What kinds of professional work have been most satisfying?

CT: I think of myself primarily as a teacher, and one reason why I've loved writing studies as a discipline is that it links pedagogy with scholarship. I have never just been an administrator and wouldn't want to be. I've had one sabbatical in my life (last year), and even then I was working with my grad students. I'm equally drawn to undergraduate and graduate teaching. In the past few years, since coming to Davis, I've been especially happy teaching science writing to our passionate, hard-working, wonderfully diverse (disciplinarily and linguistically) science majors, though I enjoy just as much the grad classes, such as the new Writing Program Administrators (WPA) course I taught for the first time last fall.

Still, I've been a WPA type for over 30 years now, and what still excites me the most about this type of program coordination is that it puts me in constant touch with people who do interesting things and are dedicated to students. I love Writing Across the

Curriculum/Writing in the Disciplines (WAC/WID) because it gets me out of a disciplinary silo and gives me a much more generous viewpoint on what's going on across the university. I always cringe when I hear people (including some folks in writing studies) bash faculty in other disciplines for being ignorant or uncaring as teachers. The people that Terry and I interviewed for *Engaged Writers and Dynamic Disciplines* were emblematic of so many teachers from different fields that I've met over the years.

The new job I took here at UC-Davis this past fall, director of our Center for Excellence in Teaching and Learning, has given me an even greater chance to find out about faculty and TAs across the whole university, and I can't begin to tell you how I've been amazed to see the inventive student-centered courses they design and how dedicated they are to teaching. We do very little of what you might call "outreach" in the center, because we have our hands full trying to facilitate the ideas and answer the questions that people bring to us. I know that this is a top-tier research university and faculty are judged on their grants and publications way more than on their teaching, so, sure, the university accommodates that agenda with quite a few overly large classes. But that makes what I'm seeing and hearing here on a daily basis all the more amazing.

CR: You mentioned in another context that you can't back-track these smart faculty teaching innovations to any programming through your Center or other WAC faculty development. Do you see evidence of a teaching culture at Davis that promotes the inventive teaching you observe? For example, do you detect a particular writing culture vis-à-vis STEM (science, technology, engineering, mathematics) departments that fosters the science writing you have been teaching yourself?

CT: My inability to back track the rise of a writing culture at Davis comes almost entirely from my still being a relative newbie here—only seven years. Our program website has an archive of documents from the early 2000s that details the reasons for the split of the writing program from English and testifies to the great respect that faculty and students across the curriculum had developed for writing and for the roles of the writing program in building it. That the archive was kept by a physicist colleague, Joe Kiskis, says something about the influence of WAC pedagogy and faculty development over the years here. One of the tasks I've undertaken since coming here has been to catalog as many of the components of that writing culture as I can observe. For example, my colleague Gary Sue Goodman and I have a piece about writing at Davis in *Writing Programs Worldwide*, and my colleague Dana Ferris and I have a somewhat historical essay on WAC and second language writers at Davis in the *Across the Disciplines* special issue on that theme.

Just last March (at 4Cs) I gave a talk specifically on the growth of a writing culture in STEM at Davis. I'd say the most profound continuing influence on that growth is the research orientation of the faculty, which includes their great respect for writing. I chaired the university committee implementing our new multi-literacies general education requirement for three years, and I was continually impressed by the ways that course proposals across disciplines, including most of the science programs, featured substantial research-related writing projects written in stages. From working with so many science majors in my courses, I can see how many opportunities advanced undergrads have to work in labs and contribute to research projects. The first time I went to the annual Undergraduate Research Conference, I was blown away by several hundred high-quality poster presentations. Similarly, I'm always impressed by the number and quality of student submissions to our annual publications *Prized Writing* and *Explorations*, about half of which come from STEM students.

That we have such a staunchly supported WAC-oriented writing program and a strong teaching center derives from this ethos, but the influences are mutually reinforcing. Students respect the writing program in part because they know they have to use what we teach in their other courses and in their careers. Reciprocally, the faculty and grad students who take advantage of WAC and teaching center workshops and consultations become better able to teach in interactive, student-centered ways.

CR: You are clearly an ace collaborator, given your publications and your ongoing mapping project of WAC programs that extends internationally. In your experience, what are the benefits of collaboration for WAC folks? Are there limitations or obstacles?

CT: For me, there's been a natural link between the collaborating I've done for years now as a WPA and the collaborative urge in scholarship and writing. I know it's not the traditional norm in the humanities, who like to hold on to that fading myth of the lone author, but collaboration is the norm in most disciplines, and to me it makes sense that two or more heads are better than one, when the goal is to pool expertise and take mutual advantage of the strengths and perspectives of others. For mature scholars, I think it's particularly important to engage graduate students in collaborations, both to give them credit for the contributions they make and to help ease them into this competitive business of publication.

In WAC/WID scholarship, I think collaboration is especially rewarding, for the co-researchers and, I'd hope, for readers. The three short texts I did for Allyn and Bacon in 1999-2000: *Writing for Psychology*, *Writing for Law Enforcement*, and *Writing about Theatre*, benefited from my working with psychologist Jim Sanford, former FBI agent John Hess, and dramaturg/producer Rick Davis. I learned so much from them and they (they said!) from me. My recent collaboration with Paula Carlino (University of Buenos Aires), Gerd Bräuer (University of Freiburg), Lisa Ganobcsik-Williams (Coventry University), and Aparna Sinha (UC-Davis) has been absolutely essential to the success of *Writing Programs Worldwide*, our new book, not to mention the contributions from our 60 authors from 28 countries. The same is true of my recent collaboration with psychologist Bob Thompson and biologist Julie Reynolds, both of Duke University, on writing in STEM, on which Julie and I (along with Pam Childers, Michael Lowry, and John Bean) presented at 4Cs in March.

Collaborative scholarship might not be everyone's cup of tea, of course. As in any relationship, there has to be a willingness to share credit and keep egos from clashing. And collaboration may be a problem for scholars in fields, including English lit, that still are not geared to understand collaboration. A good bit of that comes from the typical practice of turning dissertations (sole-authored) into books, but I can't see a good reason for persisting with a requirement for sole authorship by faculty members in some departments, when group authorship is the norm elsewhere.

CR: Ed White has often been quoted (or paraphrased) as saying that WAC programs typically undergo a boom-and-bust cycle that depends on a variety of institutional and personnel factors. Have you observed such phenomena? Do you have a model that explains how some programs succeed better or longer than others?

CT: When Tara Porter and I did the Mapping Project survey and the Cs article that grew out of it, we were conscious of Sue McLeod and Eric Miraglia's 1997 study that showed how many WAC programs depended on the longevity of an original coordinator. At our annual WAC special interest group (SIG) meetings at Cs, we hear many stories of programs that are restarting after a first effort dried up, for whatever reason. I like David Russell's explanation that WAC is precarious because it works horizontally, across traditional reporting lines in academic departments, so is not seen as part of a unit's core mission. What we saw in the Mapping Project results is that many programs have figured out ways to ensure their staying power by becoming part of the fabric of their institutions (as you and Bill Condon describe in your *CCC* article) and handling the continuity of leadership.

Tara is still in the process of mining the data for her dissertation, which is focused on this idea of sustainability, but it seems pretty clear from the data that Barbara Walvoord's advice for WAC programs to establish links with many facets of a school's operations (e.g., general education, libraries, student services, technologies, etc.) leads to sustainability. That GMU, for example, saw WAC as the model for faculty development in technology fifteen years ago and as the centerpiece of its multi-faceted assessment efforts (since 1999) ensures the prevalence of the writing culture at that university, as Terry Zawacki and I described in *Engaged Writers*.

In a different way, that the University Writing Program at Davis is its own department, with upper-level WID courses, a thriving minor, a major (in preparation), and a PhD emphasis, ensures its longevity. (By the way, five of us from the UWP are collaborating on an essay about this development for a new volume on independent writing programs.) That writing is woven throughout the general education requirements and that UWP-led writing workshops and tutoring are a major part of the Graduate School's services to students also manifest the university's writing culture. One way I'd measure the success of a WAC/WID initiative is how, over the years, a college or university culture grows that respects active learning—student proactivity in their learning, teachers creating opportunities for students to demonstrate authorship and leadership, actual participation in research teams. That Davis has had a thriving undergrad research culture for years (e.g., a prominent center, two annual publications, and several conferences) is one indication of the success of its WAC program, as are the daily pleasant surprises I get as director of the Center for Excellence in Teaching and Learning (CETL), as I mentioned above.

CR: Having collected data with your colleague Tara Porter on hundreds of WAC programs, you must have a sense of where the WAC movement, as it were, is heading in the 21st century. What are your predictions—both the fearless and reckless ones?

CT: I think about this a lot. I've just written a new version of the "WAC/WID pedagogy" chapter for the coming new edition of *A Guide to Composition Pedagogies*, plus a couple of other pieces that ask a question similar to yours. I guess that comes with being around this territory for a long time. Basically, I think WAC is here to stay, which is pretty amazing considering that we've never had our own national organization, and even our biennial conference has no ongoing organization. Yet, you'd be hard pressed to find an institution in the US that hasn't heard of it and at least thought about having a program. Even *US News* has had a category for WID since 2003—and that helps with publicity. When we started doing the research for the international portion of the Mapping Project (which led to *Writing Programs Worldwide*), we figured that "WAC" wouldn't be a well-known acronym, but I don't think I'd have qualms about that now—and that was just seven years ago.

Tara, by the way, is planning a follow-up survey, to see where we've come in the five years since we closed the US survey, but I haven't seen her design yet.

CR: Good for her. I'm eager to see that survey and participate. It sounds as though you expect the numbers of WAC programs to have increased since the first Mapping Project survey. Can you elaborate?

CT: Why am I so optimistic? Well, we are now a global information/writing-driven world in a way that we weren't when WAC began as a movement 40-plus years ago. (I was listening to National Public Radio [NPR] commentator and sardonic humorist Andrei Codrescu a while ago, and he said in his inimitable way, "I was asked for my opinion. That used to mean something, when on any issue there were three or four opinions that anyone listened to. Now everyone writes an opinion. You can't escape opinions. Everyone now has opinions on the opinions. So why should I bother?")

Moreover, as I'm learning in my new job here, teaching technologies are becoming so popular that we're close to reaching a critical mass (I don't think I'm exaggerating) in teachers' willingness to create "blended" classes (with student work going on through technologies and in classrooms) and, in more and more cases, even to "flip" the classroom—with lectures and multimedia presentations recorded for students to watch outside class, so class time can be project- and group-oriented and interactive. I won't say most courses are there yet, but the number of teachers and TAs who are moving in that direction is growing quickly. The Massive Open Online Courses (MOOC) phenomenon will cause that model to "go viral" (I hate that term), and in a few years I think it will become the norm for classes in all kinds of schools to feature much more peer-to-peer written communication, blogs, wikis, etc.—all tools that facilitate the old WAC credo of "writing to learn." It's amazing how quickly this landscape has changed. Ten years ago I'd not have ventured a statement like that.

CR: No kidding. I'm totally with you on that. And where is WAC headed?

CT: What all this means is that WAC/WID will survive and prosper not mainly because of the efforts of WAC outreach programs to convince and train teachers to be more language-centered in their teaching. That's happening because of the phenomena mentioned above. There will still be a need for teacher development and improvement, and a WAC program or a teaching center will be very helpful, even necessary, with that, but writing surely won't disappear from universities if they don't have WAC cheerleaders. But the writing and learning will be much more directed and successful with help from those organizations.

Having said all this, I get depressed thinking about a couple of forces holding back change. One is standardized assessment. The *WPA Journal* has just published my review of the excellent new book *Writing Assessment in the 21st Century* (partly a festschrift to Ed White), and it's positively scary to read the essays by folks from Educational Testing Service (ETS). They actually believe that a single instrument can capture how all these digitally and multi-modally connected young people are "writing." The ETS definition of writing is so out of date that they can't possibly be taken seriously. But the Feds and the states are handing contracts hand over fist to these people and other testing conglomerates. The result is that K-12 schools are being forced to stay frozen in time, with the further result that schools are becoming less and less relevant to the multi-modally literate kids on their smart phones and other tools outside school life. Aren't you noticing that your first-year students come in much more influenced by the literacy experience they have outside of school than in?

CR: In some ways, yes, but they are still quite constrained by expectations of them as writers in school. It's difficult for me to convince them to do something as basic as embed an image in a prose document, whereas their digital lives assume not just the skills to do that, but the necessity of illustration as part of their rhetoric.

CT: Indeed—good point. As long as writing—and every other subject in the schools—is tested by these increasingly narrow, standardized, and machine-like (and machine-readable) methods, even the most carefully-thought-out curriculum will fail to help prepare students for college—because teachers will be forced to teach to these sorry tests, which have no way to account for who our children have become in their multi-media environments.

WAC/WID is also held back by our lack of research on the increasing multi- and trans-linguality of students (and faculty), which is part of the phenomenon of global networking through technology. Only recently (e.g., the December 2011 special issue of *Across The Disciplines*, *Writing Programs Worldwide*, and a forthcoming collection co-edited by Cox and Zawacki) has the WAC scholarly community looked at how outdated a lot of "traditional" WAC pedagogy has become. At a lot of places, including Davis, we have so much work to do to incorporate policy statements like the 2009 "CCCC Statement on Second-Language Writing and Writers" into WAC/WID workshop and assessment practice. In too many places in the US, we still act as if one job of a WAC program is to help turn our students across disciplines into polished writers of standard edited American English, and to treat multilingualism as a deficit, not a strength in a global information culture.

This second concern is closely related to a third. I worry that WAC/WID—and an interdisciplinary perspective as a whole—is hindered by the continuing overemphasis in US colleges and universities, and in writing studies research, on first-year required composition courses housed in English departments. I was on the Braddock Award committee this year, and doing concentrated reading of *CCC* has sort of shocked me into seeing how the discipline of Writing Studies keeps focusing on the same—though important—US-centric, First-Year-Composition (FYC)-centric, and English-Department-centric issues that we've been writing about for decades: contingent labor in US colleges, respect for English-department-based writing programs, how writing knowledge "transfers" from FYC. In the September 2012 issue devoted to research methods, I was disappointed to see that most of the articles described varieties of archival research and text analysis, the main interests of English departments, with few pieces devoted to any methods quantitative or qualitative in relation to student development, and these only speculative.

Not being in an English department for several years now, and my currently directing a completely cross-disciplinary teaching and learning center, have given me a bit of perspective on how much WAC pedagogy and program development have been guided by the often-unconscious view that WAC is an extension of FYC, which, consciously or unconsciously, US WPAs often view as the core of writing education in higher ed. Researching structures for teaching writing around the world has shown me how US-centric that view is. Going forward, I'd like to see WAC acquire more of an international, whole university view, with language-and-learning policy seen not just in relation to the interests of FYC programs in English. This means that FYC programs and WAC programs and any other funded entities have to be accountable to the needs of the whole student and shouldn't resist (as they/we self-righteously often do) assessing their value in others' contexts.

CR: Please say more about your vision of WAC as a player in institutional transformation. Would you imagine a connection with MOOCs and other digital teaching methods?

CT: Sure. I think that's a good way to put it: WAC as a player, a significant contributor. WAC has been now for years a powerful voice at many schools, because it came along 40-plus years ago with its message of working against silo mentality and achieving linkages across the college or university. At George Mason, the success of WAC was the prototype for subsequent cross-curricular efforts, for example, in teaching with technology and innovative interdisciplinary curricula. The many people nationally who cut their teeth in WAC and then went on to other cross-disciplinary efforts or administrative posts, show that influence. And there's no reason why that influence can't continue to be powerful. The younger generation of WAC directors I've gotten to know has much the same whole-institutional vision and potential to affect transformation across their colleges and universities.

At the same time, if WAC leaders want to help change whole institutions, they have to resist equating transformation with what they know best, writing. Put another way, transforming institutions may mean not putting the WAC program first, specifically the WAC director's vision of the ideal writing-centered environment. If the only kind of transformation the WAC director wants to contribute to just realizes the goals of the WAC program, then that's not being a player, but trying to be the team. Of course, transformation can mean many things, and there are certain highly publicized "transformation" trends that WAC folks might want to resist, strenuously, such as narrow notions of assessment based on the kind of standardized testing that has so harmed K-12 education. But if the transformation we are talking about is toward a more learning-centered environment, one that appreciates the role of student thinking and creativity, then I'd think most WAC leaders could get on board with that, even if other strategies besides, or in addition to, writing are featured. That's what I've seen happening at Davis, and there is nothing in that vision incompatible with the aims of the writing program.

One transformative issue in higher ed that we all have to take seriously is scalability. Except at a few elite institutions, with very high price tags for students, student-teacher ratios have continued to climb and I doubt that will turn around. MOOCs are the (current) most extreme version of that trend, and I think we can rightly be skeptical about their potential to give students anything close to the same kind of experience that they get in a writing-rich class with 20 students or even 35 students. But we've already seen in reports from MOOC-taking students that there are some tried-and-true techniques from WAC pedagogy—specifically peer-to-peer, instructor-monitored writing forums—that can contribute to student satisfaction and deeper learning, and that are scalable in different-size venues. If we think of institutional transformation as building a more active, interactive, learning-centered environment, then we can imagine venues of different sizes that use active-learning, technology-rich techniques—some derived from WAC pedagogy—that contribute to that vision. I've worked with faculty at Davis from different fields—music, biotechnology, chemistry, sociology, etc.—who teach very large classes, even as large as 500 or more, but the size itself has not kept them from designing challenging assignments and providing useful responses, with the assistance of digital tools. Buying into scalability needn't mean riding a slippery slope to the death of small classes. Davis, for example, has many, many small capstone and research classes—that the large classes subsidize (our first-year seminars are capped at 19, for example). The students and faculty cherish these opportunities, and the balance among venues of different size enables them.

CR: Finally, is there anything you would especially want *The WAC Journal* readers to know about you, your work, or anything else?

CT: Thanks for asking, but I've gone on long enough. What a great opportunity you've given me!

Works Cited

"CCCC Statement on Second-Language Writing and Writers." Conference on College Composition and Communication. 2009. http://www.ncte.org/cccc/resources/positions/secondlangwriting.

Condon, William, and Carol Rutz. "A Taxonomy of Writing across the Curriculum Programs: Evolving to Serve Broader Agendas." *CCC*. 64.2 (2012): 357-82.

Cox, Michelle, and Terry Myers Zawacki, eds. "WAC and Second Language Writing: Crossfield Research, Theory, and Program Development." Special issue of *Across the Disciplines*. December 2011.

Elliot, Norbert, and Les Perelman, eds. *Writing Assessment in the 21st Century: Essays in Honor of Edward M. White*. New York: Hampton Press, 2012.

Ferris, Dana, and Chris Thaiss, "Writing at UC Davis: Addressing the Needs of Second Language Writers." *Across the Disciplines*. 8.4 (2011). Retrieved May 4, 2013, from http://wac.colostate.edu/atd/ell/index.cfm.

McLeod, Susan, and Eric Miraglia. "Whither WAC? Interpreting the Stories/Histories of Mature WAC Programs." *WPA*. 20.3 (1997): 46-65.

Reynolds, Julie, Christopher Thaiss, Wendy Katkin, and Robert Thompson, Jr. "Writing-to-Learn in Undergraduate Science Education: A Community-based, Conceptually Driven Approach." *CBE—Life Sciences Education*. 11: 17-25 (2012). doi:10.1187/cbe.11-08-0064 Available at http://www.lifescied.org/content/11/1/17.full

Russell, David. *Writing in the Academic Disciplines: A Curricular History*. 2nd ed. Carbondale: Southern Illinois University, 2002.

Tate, Gary, Amy Rupiper, and Kurt Schick, eds. *A Guide to Composition Pedagogies*. New York: Oxford, 2001.

Thaiss, Chris, Gerd Bräuer, Paula Carlino, Lisa Ganobcsik-Williams, and Aparna Sinha, eds. *Writing Programs Worldwide: Profiles of Academic Writing in Many Places*. Anderson, SC: Parlor Press and Fort Collins, CO: WAC Clearinghouse, 2012.

Thaiss, Chris, and Rick Davis. *Writing about Theatre*. Boston and New York: Pearson, 2000.

Thaiss, Chris, and Gary Sue Goodman. "Writing at UC Davis: Writing in Disciplines and Professions from the Undergraduate First Year through Graduate School." In Thaiss et al., eds. *Writing Programs Worldwide: Profiles of Academic Writing in Many Places* (2012): 455-66.

Thaiss, Chris, and John E. Hess. *Writing for Law Enforcement*. Boston and New York: Pearson, 2000.

Thaiss, Chris, and Tara Porter. "The State of WAC/WID in 2010: Methods and Results of the US Survey of the International WAC/WID Mapping Project." *CCC*. 61.3 (2010): 537-70.

Thaiss, Chris, and James Sanford. *Writing for Psychology*. Boston: Allyn and Bacon, 1999.

Thaiss, Chris, and Terry Myers Zawacki. *Engaged Writers and Dynamic Disciplines: Research on the Academic Writing Life*. Portsmouth, NH: Heinemann, 2006.

Walvoord, Barbara. "The Future of WAC." *College English*. 58 (1996): 58-79.

Conversations in Process: An Observational Report on WAC in China

MARTHA A. TOWNSEND AND TERRY MYERS ZAWACKI

IN MAY 2013 we co-authors found ourselves crisscrossing China at the same time, each giving invited talks at different universities about our work in writing across the curriculum and writing in the disciplines (WAC/WID).[1] Although each of us knew the other was in the country, we were there for different purposes, under different auspices and our paths did not cross. Still, we believe our collective experiences contribute first-hand observations that further contextualize the research Wu Dan writes about in *Introducing Writing Across the Curriculum into China: Feasibility and Adaptation* (2012), reviewed in this volume. We both served as informants to Wu Dan as she was doing her dissertation research, on which the book is based, and we both met with her (though on different days) at Xi'an International Studies University where she now teaches when we were in China. Our observations, although derived from only the six institutions we visited, help document a growing interest in WAC in China as well as a desire on the part of the faculty with whom we met for an ongoing cross-national dialogue among Chinese and US scholars on writing instruction across the disciplines.

This article is based mainly on conversations with EFL faculty, administrators and students during our visits to universities that have varying educational missions, ranging from science and technology, teacher education, international studies and a "Sino-Foreign" English-medium collaboration (see Appendix for list of institutions). On our return to the US we spent a day together discussing what we had seen and learned about the state of postsecondary EFL writing instruction and WAC in mainland China,[2] gradually narrowing our focus to themes and issues we thought most pressing in light of the increasing numbers of Chinese international students we are encountering in our US composition and WID courses. These include the influence of a national testing culture on approaches to writing instruction, particularly the use of formulaic, decontextualized assignments to demonstrate learning rather than the use of writing to aid learning; faculty and students' understandings of and expectations for critical and original thinking; and concerns about maintaining Chinese rhetorical traditions when Western-style writing is increasingly the goal whether students are writing for specific purposes in English or in Chinese. Our observations here join with conversations in progress, conversations evidenced in recent articles in *College Composition and Communication* and *College English*, new books found on the WAC Clearinghouse and articles by Chinese scholars in the *Writing Research Across Borders* (WRAB) volumes, among other publications. The first half of our essay presents some of the literature that we searched in preparation for our 2013 visits, supplemented with related observations and reflections. The second half addresses the themes and issues noted above that emerged for us as a result of our visits and subsequent conversations. We close with news of nascent but promising WAC efforts that are underway now.

By way of background, we note that both of us have a longstanding interest in and experience with international applications of writing instruction through our US professional activities, our scholarship, and our travels abroad.[3] More than a decade ago, for example, Marty wrote about the ways writing is part of the teaching and learning environment at Nankai University, a well-respected research university in Tianjin (2002). Based on the first of Marty's three WAC-related China visits, this first article details her interviews with faculty, alumnae, and students about their university writing experiences. These interviews, conducted in 1999, were very much on Marty's mind during the visit that is written about in this article. For a second visit in 2007, she served on the US steering committee to plan and host "Literacies of Hope: Making Meaning across Boundaries," an academic conference that brought together Chinese and American scholars at Beijing Normal University, China's premier institution for teacher education. Both Marty's 1999 and 2013 visits were sponsored by the University of Missouri's Council on International Initiatives, which supports faculty in international teaching and research.

Terry's visit to China was arranged by Wu Dan and by Liu Xinghua at Shanghai Jiaotong University, whom Terry had first met at a European writing research conference in Prague where she was an invited presenter. While Terry's China visit was her first, she has traveled several times to the Middle East to give talks and work with faculty and administrators on implementing WAC at postsecondary institutions in the United Arab Emirates and Qatar. In both the Middle East and in China, the focus of the invited workshops and talks Terry gave was on writing and teaching writing across the curriculum in English as a second language. We want to note, however, that Arab and Chinese scholars in these countries are also increasingly engaged in research on L1 (first language) academic writing practices in the disciplines. We point, for example, to Chen Huijun's "Modern 'Writingology' in China" (2010), in which she describes the rise of interest in and research on "practical" or applied writing in Chinese postsecondary language instruction. Our visits in 2013 however, connected us with composition and WAC-interested Chinese colleagues in EFL fields, so that is our focus here.

Brief Bibliographic Background, with Commentary

Our description of the Chinese EFL literature we consulted is both brief and selective; we aim to introduce readers to fairly new work we believe is especially interesting and informative. In general, we find limited publications in English on postsecondary EFL writing studies and/or writing in and across disciplines by Chinese scholars working in China. There is, however, a larger body of work on L2 (second language) writing available in Chinese. This is not surprising since even if Chinese scholars have been educated in English-medium institutions, they are expected to publish their research in Chinese in Chinese journals to be considered for promotion (Wu Dan email communication 15 December 2010).[4] Whether writing in Chinese or in English, the authors typically have backgrounds in applied linguistics or translation studies; those writing in English are generally publishing in TESOL, EAP or ESP journals.[5]

We begin by referring readers to Mya Poe's review of Wu Dan's *Introducing Writing Across the Curriculum into China* (2013). Based on her dissertation research at Clemson University under the direction of Art Young, Wu Dan's book is the first full-length consideration of WAC's potential contribution to higher education in China. She makes a compelling case that China needs WAC and that the time is right given the current national attention to the quality of teaching and learning in higher education; yet, as she told us, her book is mostly unknown in China and print copies are not yet available to Chinese readers. Beyond Poe's review, we note from our (separate) conversations with Wu Dan that faculty attitudes about student writing and teaching with writing in the disciplines that she describes are very much like our own in the US but are exacerbated because cross-discipline and cross-departmental—not to mention cross-institutional—communication between faculty in China is rare. Few channels exist for faculty exchange or conversation around writing, such as US faculty might have through centers for teaching and learning. Departments and colleagues seem isolated from one another; the writing center, for example, at Wu Dan's institution, Xi'an International Studies University, is open only to English majors. She herself was transferred from English Studies to the School of International Programs because it was believed that she could provide more help to students with her knowledge of American higher education. Yet this move further isolated her from other departments and has hampered her WAC efforts (although she did design and teach a WAC-focused graduate course for the English Studies department).

We also refer readers to a recent special issue of *College English*, "Studying Chinese Rhetoric in the Twenty-First Century," edited by LuMing Mao (2010). As Mao writes in his introduction, the five articles in this special issue are intended to complicate what has often been characterized in the literature as the East-West cultural and rhetorical divide; rather, he hopes to "negotiate between developing a localized narrative and searching for its broader significance without turning it into a super narrative" (p. 341). We hope to contribute to that same cause with this article.

Composition scholars may already be familiar with the recent *CCC* article "College Writing in China and America: A Modest and Humble Conversation, with Writing Samples" by Patrick Sullivan, Yufeng Zhang, and Fenglan Zheng (2012). Here, three teacher-researchers, one American and two Chinese, read and responded to essays written by students in China and the US. The authors conclude that, while there are marked differences in both the student writing and teachers' responses to the writing, these differences stem not solely from different rhetorical traditions but also from a very different view of the role of writing in student learning—that is, whether writing is viewed as a way to learn or a way to demonstrate learning. Zhoulin Ruan, one of the faculty who hosted Terry's visit, discusses this pedagogical divide in *Metacognitive Knowledge in Self-regulated Language Learning and Writing* (2012). He explains that while Chinese EFL teachers are familiar with process pedagogies and socially-situated approaches to teaching writing, these are far from being widely adopted in writing classes that are generally still taught along current-traditional lines, largely in response to China's emphasis on testing, a point we comment on more fully below.[6] One of the questions for Ruan, then, is how an awareness of task, purpose, audience and cross-cultural rhetorical preferences might help to foster Chinese students' autonomy as writers.

Increasingly, Chinese scholars are arguing for more contextualized approaches to researching and teaching writing.[7] In "More than Ba Gu Wen (Eight-legged Essay) and Confucianism: A New Research Agenda for English-Chinese Writing Studies," Xinghua Liu (2011), another of Terry's hosts, calls for an ecological approach that considers the nature and "academic domain" (discipline) of the writing task, the students' L1 and L2 educational and writing backgrounds, and their perceptions of their own processes and difficulties (p. 5). Similarly, Xiao Lei (2008), in "Exploring a Sociocultural Approach to Writing Strategy Research: Mediated Actions in Writing Activities," argues that cognition and content are so deeply interrelated that to study cognition one must look at sociocultural contexts and the activity systems in which writing occurs. She also acknowledges however, the complex role language acquisition plays as a fundamental element of context. An overarching question asked by faculty at all of the universities where Terry spoke was how to balance attention to disciplinary and rhetorical contexts in their English L2 writing instruction when students are still struggling to acquire fluency and accuracy at the sentence level. This question is, of course, one that Chinese writing instructors will need to grapple with if WAC pedagogies are introduced, although they will find precedent in the numerous places in the US where WAC has been applied to foreign language instruction.

At the same time that many Chinese English L2 writing scholars are making arguments for more situated approaches to writing research and teaching, they also note the powerful effects of the required national tests of English on writing instruction. In their surveys of K-12 Chinese teachers of English, Danling Fu and Marylou Matoush (2012) found that high school and college entrance exams not only drive writing instruction but also shape the attitudes of students and parents who see English writing as the application of correct vocabulary and form and very much isolated from the rhetorical traditions of their Chinese L1. In *Writing in the Devil's Tongue: A History of English Composition in China*, Xiaoye You (2010) describes the role of writing and national examinations in traditional Chinese education and the changes that occurred with the "infiltration" of Western rhetoric (among other influences) from the late 1800s through to the present. His chapters on the continued influence of traditional rhetorical forms, the introduction of expressivist and process pedagogies in the 60s and 70s, and the persistent formulaic constraints imposed by the required College English Test (CET) provide a valuable guide to understanding the "global contact zone" (p. 175) of postsecondary English writing instruction in China.

Also valuable is a new book on the WAC Clearinghouse, *Chinese Rhetoric and Writing: An Introduction for Language Teachers* in which Andy Kirkpatrick and Zhichang Xu (2012) trace the development of Chinese rhetorical traditions. They argue that Chinese writing styles are dynamic and changing in response to sociopolitical contexts, just as other languages are. To suggest, as many scholars have, that Chinese students bring "culturally determined and virtually ineradicable rhetorical traditions to their English writing" is to overlook that fact. Yet, the authors argue, writing teachers should not aim "to gut the English of the Chinese writer of local cultural and rhetorical influences," but to see how students can draw on these influences to form effective texts (p. 4).[8]

You's and Kirkpatrick and Xu's insistence on the importance of recognizing and valuing differences—historical, cultural, rhetorical, pedagogical—in the Chinese/Western encounter returns us to the article Marty wrote over ten years ago, "Writing in/across the Curriculum at a Comprehensive Chinese University" (2002), in which she reports on interviews with twenty-five faculty, students, and alumnae of Nankai University. The goal was to discover whether an instructional initiative comparable to WAC in the US might exist at Nankai. Equal in importance to the research findings, however, are the essay's cautions for US WAC professionals, two of which are particularly pertinent here; summarized these are:

- American-style WAC pedagogies cannot and should not be promulgated uncritically in other cultures.
- Social, economic, historic, political, and institutional pressures mitigate against acceptance and success of US-style WAC pedagogies in China. In particular, although American educators associate WAC pedagogies with critical thinking (in the form of encouraging students to question texts), Chinese faculty and students are not rewarded for challenging authority.

As we look at this article again, we are struck by the prescience of these cautions, especially in light of current arguments around translingualism and global Englishes. (See, for example, Canagarajah and Horner, et al.).

Emergent Themes and Questions Raised

Given the recent attention to rhetorical traditions and writing instruction in China, coupled with the interest in English L2 writing studies as shown in the literature above, we might have expected to encounter faculty with knowledge about WAC during our 2013 visits. Yet, apart from Wu Dan's monograph and our hosts' stated interest after our presentations, we found but scant knowledge of WAC during our professional travels.

What we did find is uncannily close to the displeasure that US compositionists endured for years prior to the introduction of WAC here—and in some places still do. The English language teachers Marty spoke with in China, for example, frequently commented that their discipline-based colleagues are asking, "Why haven't you taught our students to write better? They took your courses, so why are they producing such poor scientific papers for us?" In her research, Wu Dan reports similar comments as well, such as Chinese colleagues noting that writing skills are very important but that they have neither the time nor knowledge to teach these skills.

We suspect that Chinese discipline-based teachers' reluctance to engage with students' writing traces not only to their reported lack of time and knowledge but also to the relative lower importance of written work compared with the culture of national examinations. For example, Chinese students in many disciplines at both the undergraduate and graduate levels are expected to produce an independently written "scientific paper" based on research in their respective fields as a requirement for graduation. "Scientific" in this context does not refer to science *per se*. Rather, it means a student-researched paper produced in any discipline as a threshold or high stakes document that demonstrates the student's ability to think, research, and solve problems in his or her academic field. Typically, undergraduate students begin research for this paper in their third year and continue on into their final year—at the end of which they "write it up." At one institution, Marty was told of students being allowed to graduate with papers still unfinished; even though the research was concluded, the final document was incomplete and numerous exceptions were being made so students could graduate. Although professors guide their students through the necessary steps for research, guidance on writing the paper, she was told, is minimal. We wonder whether demonstrating the ability to do the research is paramount and that forging that research into a written document is not as crucial.

We also suspect the experience reported by Yaoqui Zhou, an informatics scholar at Indiana University's School of Medicine, might be typical of faculty who see writing mainly as a product rather than what it might demonstrate about learning. (Our using an example from science to illustrate the point above about "scientific" papers is coincidental.) In the introduction to a set of guidelines Zhou produced for the graduate students working in his Indiana University lab, Zhou says that even though he had more than twenty publications by the time he had earned his PhD at SUNY-Stony Brook, his understanding of how to write a high-quality paper "remained at an elementary level and was limited to minimization of grammatical errors." He had simply accepted his advisors' corrections without asking what they meant. Later, during postdoctoral work at North Carolina State University, his mentor suggested that he attend a two-day workshop on writing at nearby Duke University. Zhou writes: "The workshop taught by Professor Gopen truly opened my eyes. For the first time, I learned that readers have expectations when they read, and the most effective way to write is to fulfill their expectations. . . . [I came to] realize that a good paper requires an in-depth, tough, and thorough self-review." Zhou's reference to George Gopen's work will not surprise WAC scholars in the US and Zhou's guidelines for his own students, based on Gopen's workshop and offered in both English and Chinese PDF versions, represent an admirable attempt to "pay forward" the rhetorical understandings he wants his own students to demonstrate in their writing.

Given the comments made to both of us by the EFL teachers we met, they would welcome knowledge of the WAC research and work that has gone on in the US for over thirty years now. After Marty's presentations about the underlying principles of WAC, with selected examples of classroom application, teachers expressed a sense of liberation in learning that they, in fact, are not responsible for Chinese students' "poor" writing in discipline-based classes. When WAC theory and concepts are explained, interest is robust. After her lectures, Terry, too, heard faculty say, "This needs to be a discussion here."

And there is much to discuss, as we recognized while outlining this article. These include questions that Marty encountered when she spoke about the importance of writing to learn along with writing to demonstrate learning in courses across the curriculum. And questions that Terry was asked when she talked about her research with international students in the US, in particular, the difficulties they report with faculty demands for originality and critical thinking. During Terry's China presentations, she observed graduate students and faculty nodding in agreement, especially in response to her comment that Chinese international students she interviewed for her WAC and second language research all said that they regretted losing the "beauty" of their language as they learned to conform to US teachers' expectations.

We turn first to Marty's experience when she demonstrated several examples of how short, low-stakes writing-to-learn assignments might enhance students' understanding of difficult course concepts—and help them be more prepared to tackle the rigorous demands of their longer, high-stakes writing assignments to come. While some Chinese faculty seemed familiar with the idea, they indicated that so-called "writing to learn" practices are not widely used; some questioned why students would do them, if they were not receiving a grade. In one middle school English class that Marty was invited to observe, approximately sixty students were crowded shoulder-to-shoulder into a classroom at long, narrow tables, facing one another over rows of stacked books. A young teacher read short passages from a text, after which students quietly circled multiple-choice answers in printed workbooks. No teacher-student interaction occurred, and students did not have an opportunity to speak about what they were hearing. More to the point, judging from class size and reliance on the texts provided, students would not be writing short passages of their own in response to the reading.

The school Marty visited, with more than 7,600 residential students who live in dormitories and return home only on weekends, was selected because of its status as a "Provincial Model Unit in Moral Standards,"[9] one to which the county government "gives priority to the development of education" and thus significant resources. The school places "ultra emphasis on scientific management, and deepens classroom teaching reform." Administrators, including the full-time on-site Party Leader, proudly describe the school's audio-visual and other "experimental devices," high quality teaching staff, science labs, ten computer classrooms and one-hundred-thousand-book library. Even though observing the class only briefly, Marty wondered how much these students' acquisition of English (or any other subject) might improve if they were writing just occasional short paragraphs. The scene recalled You's conclusion in "The choice made from no choice": "[S]tudents' individual needs for English are hardly acknowledged; many teachers are predominantly concerned about teaching language knowledge and test-taking skills, instead of language skills for communication purposes. English writing is still taught in the current-traditional approach, focusing on correct form rather than helping the students develop thoughts" (108).

We surmise that Chinese teachers' reluctance to embrace writing-to-learn pedagogies is closely tied to the well-established testing culture that dominates all levels of education, as mentioned earlier. As Ze Wang, Xiao Yong Hu, and Yong Yu Guo explain in "Goal Contents and Goal Contexts: Experiments with Chinese Students" (2012), the pursuit of scholarship as a means of attaining economic well-being and social status is inextricably interwoven in Chinese history and culture. Drawing on previous studies by other scholars, they show that official examinations of scholarly learning in China trace to 700 AD. They write, "High-stakes testing, high educational expectations from parents, traditional values, and teaching practices that make comparisons transparent (e.g., test scores or rankings made public to all teachers and/or students) contribute to a competitive school environment in China, even in middle schools" (p. 108).

It is easy to see that an examination system that values standardized testing to the degree that China's does will not readily embrace writing that does not *demonstrate* knowledge but only leads *toward* it. In "The Education System That Pulled China Up May Now Be Holding It Back" (2012), Helen Gao describes how disorienting it was for her to come to the US for study after having had an education that prepared her primarily for taking the *gaokao*, China's annual, nationwide college entrance exam. In an "intense, memorization-heavy" nine-hour exam over two days, during which city neighborhoods near testing sites virtually shut down, students provide rote answers to mostly multiple-choice machine-graded questions. Gao's education had not prepared her for the analytic essays she subsequently encountered in the US. Lest we seem to appear too US-centric in this observation, however, we hasten to point out that WAC pedagogies may prove to be part of the answer to enabling Chinese students in our classrooms—whether in China or the US—to make sense of writing assignments they encounter as English L2 learners. Pedagogies that call for incremental development of longer papers, multiple drafts with revision based on feedback from teachers, and explicit grading criteria—the staples of WAC—may go a long way toward diffusing Chinese students' confusion.

This is not to say, however, that, even with attention to writing processes, students—and teachers—will not be confused about other US-centric values, as was apparent in the questions Terry was asked, for example, about expectations for critical thinking and originality in writing. Both of these concepts seem particularly troublesome to understand and enact in a Chinese context for many reasons, cultural and linguistic.[10] An article given to Terry by Lihong Wang, a visiting scholar with whom she met at George Mason prior to her trip to China, is especially useful in helping to understand that context. In "'But when you are doing your exams it is the same as in China'—Chinese Students Adjusting to Western Approaches to Teaching and Learning," Wang, who did her doctoral work in the UK, cautions against making easy comparisons between Chinese and Western educational practices, such as seeing memorization as exclusive of understanding or as synonymous with rote learning in contrast to thinking critically. As Wang's and others' investigations show, both Chinese students and teachers see memorization and understanding as "interlocking processes, complementary to each other" and achieved with "considerable mental effort" rather than "a process of sudden insight" (p. 408). Wang calls this belief "effortful learning/*kuxin*," or the idea that "painstaking effort" is required for all learning. This "inherited" belief goes along with two others—"reflective learning/*yong xin*," which requires "emotional and intellectual commitment" and "humble learning/*xu xin*," which emphasizes "learning from others with modesty and humility" (p. 410-13). Yet "humble learning," as we see from so much of the literature on Asian students' writing, often seems in direct opposition to our Western conceptions of critical thinking and the need for students to learn to generate original arguments.

We do not mean to imply, however, that Chinese students are not expected to think critically. Western-style critical thinking was mentioned as an expectation by the EFL faculty with whom we talked but also something which many felt was particularly difficult to teach—given, as we noted earlier, the pervasive testing culture and students' ongoing struggles to articulate complex knowledge in English. On the other hand, when students become more acclimated to writing in English, as Wang's research shows and as Terry could clearly see from the graduate and advanced undergraduate students she talked to, they are quite able to adapt to teachers' expectations for thinking originally and critically. Two of the undergraduates Terry met at the English-medium institution she visited, for example, described enthusiastically the assignment they were working on for a web-based marketing plan for Apple that was sensitive to Chinese contexts.

The students' demonstrated ability to adapt to Western rhetorical norms, however, begs the question of whether and the extent to which they should. Zhoulin Ruan, whose book we referenced earlier and who has published numerous articles on critical thinking, expressed some concern to Terry about the Chinese rhetorical traditions that are being lost with the national emphasis on learning to write in English. Terry found this a striking but perhaps not surprising observation coming from someone who is the head of the Department of English, Culture and Communication at Xi'an Jiaotong-Liverpool University, an English-medium institution, and whose scholarship concerns metacognition and self-regulated language learning and writing.

Promising Signs for WAC in China—What We Are Seeing Now

Based on conversations with WAC-interested faculty and administrators both in China and on our return, we see many promising—and exciting—signs for the start of WAC in China. We begin with the "needs assessment" survey research Wu Dan conducted to determine whether students in different departments would like to see a bilingual writing center established for all students. Students responded that they need and want assistance with writing in both Chinese and English, so the next step for Wu Dan, as she wrote to us, is to report her findings to the university administration to begin a conversation about both Chinese and English writing across the curriculum. Given the current national emphasis on evaluating instructional quality in higher education and a first-round governmental report indicating that much improvement is necessary, Wu Dan anticipates that the university administration will be receptive to the idea of WAC. "If WAC can be introduced to institutions as one possible method to help teaching and learning," she writes, "or be used as 'proof' that the university has tried to work on instructional quality, then the national evaluations are actually good opportunities for WAC to be started in China" (email communication 5 August 2013). In addition, both Ruan and Liu agreed that WAC is "an important future direction of English L2 writing teaching and research in China considering the current transition from college English teaching to English for Specific Purposes" (Liu, email communication 2 August 2013).

We also see exciting potential in the listserv Ruan is developing with assistance from Wu Dan and Liu as a platform for conversations among WAC-interested faculty. In his initial posting on this planned WAC network, Ruan writes that "Such a forum will enable us to discuss some key issues in teaching and research on WAC in China; explore the potential of research collaborations across different institutions; organize WAC seminars and symposiums in China; develop a Chinese association of WAC when it matures; establish a collective connection with the international community of WAC; etc. etc. . ."[11] (email communication 1 August 2013). To support these efforts, we note here that Mike Palmquist has extended invitations to Zhoulin Ruan and Wu Dan to join the WAC Clearinghouse Publications Review Board, a move that recognizes these scholars' WAC interests and moreover makes their expertise visible to their colleagues in China.

In a timely confluence of events for WAC in China, Marty learned just prior to her trip that one of the US's most prominent WAC resources—John Bean's first edition of *Engaging Ideas* (1996)—is available in Chinese translation. Of the translation's origin, John tells us that "about ten or twelve years ago, I gave a WAC workshop at the University of Wyoming and a Chinese professor in the Department of Agriculture—Rhenduo Zhang—asked if he could translate the book into Chinese. He handled all the details and produced the translation surprisingly fast" (email communication 15 May 2013). John does not know to what extent the book has been used, although Martha Patton, newly retired from her English position at Missouri and now teaching English through the Peace Corps at Southwest University's School of Foreign Languages in Chongqing, told us that she has forwarded her only copy of the Chinese translation to her dean, who is "interested in these ideas, does want to make changes, and is beginning to implement some" (email communication 16 May 2013). We also know that two of the faculty Marty worked with at Northwest University of Agriculture and Forestry have obtained the book in Chinese. If the concepts in *Engaging Ideas* prove adaptable by the Chinese professoriate and the book has a fraction of the impact in China that it has had on the American professoriate, WAC may begin to achieve what WU Dan calls for in *Introducing Writing Across the Curriculum Into China*.

Conclusion: Where Can We in the US Go From Here?

While this essay is not a formal study by either of us and is based on a limited sample of institutions, we believe our observations point to exciting possibilities for WAC in China. Both our formal presentations and informal interactions with Chinese colleagues generated genuine interest in the WAC work being done by US scholars; we, likewise, have much to learn from them. Toward that end, we encourage WAC scholars to become familiar with the literature on writing in China; to take time to talk with visiting colleagues from China about their work; to volunteer to host Chinese scholars if opportunity arises (Marty, for example, will be hosting two scholars from Northwest University of Agriculture and Forestry in the 2013–2014 academic year and may return to NUAF to teach a short seminar); to welcome visiting Chinese scholars into their graduate seminars; and to engage Chinese graduate students in study of WAC, as Art Young did at Clemson with Wu Dan. However, mindful of the cautions we mentioned earlier, we call for a genuine exchange of research and practice, an exchange that values the rich rhetorical history and traditions of teaching writing in China.

It seems appropriate, then, to close our observations with the Chinese term 接轨 or *jiegui,* which is often used to refer to acts of dialogue and connection (literally "connecting the tracks"), to say how exciting it is to be playing some small role in connecting WAC-interested Chinese scholars to one another and to WAC scholars in the US with the goal of sharing research and pedagogies across our borders.

Acknowledgments

Marty thanks Michael J. O'Brien, Dean of Arts and Science, and the MU Council on International Initiatives for supporting her participation in the University of Missouri's 2013 Global Scholars Program. Terry thanks Wu Dan and Liu Xinghua, who organized and sponsored her visits within China, and Zhoulin Ruan, who hosted her visit to Suzhou and arranged for her to spend time with three very impressive undergraduate students.

Notes

1. For simplicity's sake, we use "WAC" to refer to both WAC and WID throughout this essay, intending for readers to assume an expanded definition of both terms in the single label. In fact, we conflate the meanings of both in our work and, in most cases, find using separate terms misleading and unnecessary.

2. Our interactions with Chinese scholars, and our comments in this article, are limited to mainland China. The educational system in Hong Kong, a Chinese SAR (special administrative region), developed under British rule and its writing instruction has evolved in concert with British traditions.

3. See Notes on Contributors in this issue for more details on our professional activities and scholarship related to our broader international WAC experiences.

4. After having her article accepted for a "WAC and Second Language Writing" special issue of *Across the Disciplines* that Terry co-edited, Wu Dan had to withdraw when she was told by her supervisors that the publication would not count for promotion and that she "should try to translate it into Chinese for a Chinese journal." In a more recent email, Wu Dan confirmed this point, adding that she will present "Missing persons: The under/unrepresented writers and readers in English L2 writing studies research in China" at the 2013 Symposium on Second Language Writing in Shandong, China. Her paper includes a review of second-language (L2) writing studies in China, "*almost all of which are in Chinese [her emphasis]*" (email communication 4 August 2013).

5. EAP, or English for Academic Purposes, and ESP, English for Specific Purposes, are the closest academic constructs in China and many other countries to the US initiatives for WAC, WID, CXC, ECAC, and the like. EAP and ESP often take the form of stand-alone programs or are combined with some version of teaching and learning resource centers.

6. In "'The choice made from no choice': English Writing Instruction in a Chinese University" (2003), Xiaoye You investigates the often uncritical transplantation of Western writing pedagogies into first and second-year classes designed for non-English majors, classes that are taught under a system requiring teachers to prepare students for China's national examination system. This requirement leads to a focus on correct form rather than on language for communication, even when teachers are versed in process and expressivist pedagogies.

7. Arguments are being made for applied or contextualized writing instruction in both Chinese and English writing studies, at least partly in response to national directives, as Huijun explains in "Modern 'Writingology' in China."

8. We also see this attention to China's rhetorical traditions in the writing of two popular contemporary authors, one Chinese and one American, both of whom should be read by scholars seeking to understand Chinese language and culture. Yu Hua is among China's top

contemporary writers; his newest work, *China in Ten Words* (2011), combines memoir with social commentary. Each of the ten one-word-titled chapters is based on a mandarin character that Hua believes describes the country today. The chapters "Reading" and "Writing" are particularly relevant for our community. In *Oracle Bones* (2007), American journalist Peter Hessler employs an archeological framework, both literal and figurative, to explore China's changing cultural landscape; the title itself refers to characters inscribed on shell and bone, thought to be the earliest known writing in East Asia. That these characters can still be read by modern Chinese readers, even though modern characters are vastly more sophisticated, is one of the reasons, Hessler explains, that the character writing system and the beauty of the characters themselves are so deeply embedded in Chinese culture and identity.

9. Quotations here are taken from printed material provided by the school. The school's designation as locus for students' moral development traces to Confucian philosophy that holds that the state is the moral guardian of the people (Asia for Educators). As we note elsewhere in this article, China's standardized exam system is related to this concept as well.

10. Teachers' expectations for originality are also among the most fraught for English L1 students as Chris Thaiss and Terry found in their research for *Engaged Writers and Dynamic Disciplines*.

11. We are thrilled to be included in these early efforts at building a WAC network and are being copied on the messages, as is Mike Palmquist.

Works Cited

"Asia for Educators." Columbia University. 2013. Web. 17 Sept. 2013.

Bean, J. C. (2011). *Engaging Ideas: The Professor's Guide to Integrating Writing, Critical Thinking, and Active Learning in the Classroom*. Chinese Translation. San Francisco: Jossey-Bass.

Canagarajah, A. S. (2006). The place of world Englishes in composition: Pluralization continued. *College Composition and Communication*, 57(4), 586-619.

Fu, D. & Matoush, M. (2012). Teachers' perceptions of English language writing instruction in China. In C. Bazerman et al (Eds.), *International Advances in Writing Research: Cultures, Places, Measures*. (23-40). Perspectives on Writing. Fort Collins, Colorado: The WAC Clearinghouse and Parlor Press. Available at http://wac.colostate.edu/books/wrab2011/.

Gao, H. (2012). The education system that pulled china up may now be holding it back. *The Atlantic*. Available at http://www.theatlantic.com/international/2012/06/the-education-system-that-pulled-china-up-may-now-be-holding-it-back/258787/

Hessler, P. (2006). *Oracle Bones: A Journey through Time in China*. NY: Harper Collins.

Horner, B., Lu, M-Z, Royster, J. J., & Trimbur, J. (2011). A translingual approach to language difference in writing. *College English*, 73(3), 303-21

Hua, Y. (2011). *China in Ten Words*. New York: Pantheon Books.

Huijun, C. (2010). Modern "writingology" in China. In C. Bazerman et al. (Eds.), *Traditions of Writing Research*. (3-16). NY: Routledge.

Kirkpatrick, A. & Xu, Z. (2012). *Chinese Rhetoric and Writing: An Introduction for Language Teachers*. Fort Collins, Colorado: The WAC Clearinghouse and Parlor Press. Available at http://wac.colostate.edu/books/kirkpatrick_xu/.

Lei, X. (2008). Exploring a sociocultural approach to writing strategy research: Mediated actions in writing activities. *Journal of Second Language Writing* 17, 217-236.

Liu, X. (2010). More than ba gu wen (eight-legged essay) and Confuciansim: A new research agenda for English-Chinese writing studies. *SLW News: The Newsletter of Second Language Writing Interest Section*. PDF at http://newsmanager.commpartners.com/tesol-slwis/print/2011-11-30/1.html. Retrieved 3 July 2012.

Mao, L. (2010). Introduction. Searching for the way: Between the whats and wheres of Chinese rhetoric. *College English*, 72(4), 329-249.

Ruan, Z. (2012). *Metacognitive Knowledge in Self-regulated Language Learning and Writing*. Shanghai Foreign Language Press. Print. Book information at www.sflep.com.

Sullivan, P., Zhang, Y. & Zheng, F. (2012). College writing in China: A modest and humble conversation with writing samples. *College Composition and Communication*, 64(2), 306-31.

Thaiss, C. & Zawacki, T. (2006). *Engaged Writers and Dynamic Disciplines: Research on the Academic Writing Life*. Portsmouth, NH: Boynton/Cook.

Townsend, M. A. (2002). Writing in/across the curriculum at a comprehensive Chinese university. *Language & Learning Across the Disciplines* 5(3), 134-49.

Wang, L. (2011). "But when you are doing your exams it is the same as in China": Chinese students adjusting to western approaches to teaching and learning. *Cambridge Journal of Education* 41(4), 407-24.

Wang, Z, Hu, X, & Guo, Y. Y. (2012). Goal contents and goal contexts; Experiments with Chinese Students. *The Journal of Experimental Education* 81(1), 105-22.

Wu, Dan. (2013). *Introducing Writing Across the Curriculum into China: Feasibility and Adaptation*. Heidelberg: Springer.

You, X. (2003). "The choice made from no choice": English writing instruction in a Chinese University. *Journal of Second Language Writing* (13), 97-110.

You, X. (2010). *Writing in the Devil's Tongue: A History of English Composition in China*. Carbondale: Southern Illinois University Press.

Zhou, Y. "Recipe for a quality scientific paper: Fulfill readers' and reviewers' expectations." 19 June 2007. PDF at http://sparks.informatics.iupui.edu/Publications_files/write-english.php retrieved 4 August 2013.

Appendix: Universities Townsend and Zawacki visited in 2013

Shanghai Normal University, Fengxian & Xuhui campuses, May 18 – 21 (MT)
Shandong University of Technology, Zibo, May 23 – 24 (MT)
Northwest University of Agriculture and Forestry, Yangling, May 26 – 27 (MT)
Xi'an International Studies University, Xi'an, May 22-24 (TZ)
Shanghai Jiaotong University, Shanghai, May 29 (TZ)
Xi'an Jiaotong-Liverpool University, Suzhou, May 30. (TZ)

Review

MYA POE

Dan, Wu. *Introducing Writing Across the Curriculum into China: Feasibility and Adaptation.* New York: Springer, 2013. 150 pages.

INTRODUCING WRITING ACROSS THE CURRICULUM INTO CHINA: Feasibility and Adaptation is an offering in the Springer Briefs in Education series, which are manuscripts published as part of Springer's eBook Collection and available for individual print purchase. Manuscripts in the Spring Briefs series combine elements of journals and books, presenting "concise summaries of cutting-edge research and practical applications in education" (Springer). I was eager to read *Introducing Writing Across the Curriculum into China* and can recommend the book because of the perspective it offers on the potential of Writing Across the Curriculum (WAC) in China.

Introducing Writing Across the Curriculum into China, which closely follows Wu Dan's 2010 dissertation from Clemson University, includes seven chapters with the first three chapters providing introductory material and historical framing. Chapter four is dedicated to methods—interviews of twenty-eight Chinese university faculty, administrators, and recruiters from "state-owned, foreign or joint, and private companies" (48) and interviews of eight leading US WAC scholars. Chapters five and six offer interview results, divided into findings from Chinese participants and findings from US participants. Based on those interview results, Wu Dan derives the opportunities and challenges for introducing WAC into mainland Chinese higher education. The book concludes with a summary of her feasibility analysis, suggesting, for example, that WAC initiatives in China might bring together internationally-trained writing researchers, Chinese literature teachers, English language teachers, and faculty in the disciplines to expand the reach of WAC beyond English-language instruction: "WAC programs in China quite possibly will be initiated by [US trained

Chinese writing researchers] with an initial focus on English writing but will be eventually expanded to Chinese writing" (113).

The introductory material and historical framing provide a review of the WAC movement in the US and description of changes to Chinese higher education. As readers of *The WAC Journal* will know, origin narratives of WAC in the US have been a staple of WAC scholarship since the 1980s. While most articles today no longer need to recount early programs at Carleton College and Beaver College or theoretical distinctions between WAC and Writing in the Disciplines (WID), the story of how WAC came to a specific institution remains an important element in much scholarship still found in the field. Likewise, more recent scholarship has tended to point to where WAC is going, especially in regards to technological advances as well as support for graduate students and multilingual writers. And, importantly, Chris Thaiss's WAC WID Mapping Project has made us cognizant of the international spread of WAC or WAC-like initiatives. Wu Dan's book adds much needed details about the possibilities for introducing WAC into China (hence, the title of the book). In doing so, she lays the groundwork for an origin narrative of WAC in China with provocative suggestions for the possibilities as well as challenges of introducing and sustaining WAC initiatives in mainland China. (Wu Dan notes that WAC interventions to date have been at sites such as Hong Kong and Taiwan, which have different political, colonial, and linguistic histories than mainland China.)

Such narratives are important in contemporary international WAC scholarship for several reasons. First, they give us a portrait of the history of higher education in other national contexts. As Wu Dan explains, the Chinese higher education system is "a combination of an indigenous tradition that can be traced to 135 BCE and an imported Western model" (p. 28). The modern Chinese higher education system has a relatively short history that has been punctuated with dramatic ideological and curricular shifts. For instance, after World War II, Chinese culture underwent a massive upheaval with the introduction of Soviet-style education: "in the Soviet model, higher education faculty and students were assigned to specialized institutions, each focusing on one area, creating a planned workforce to serve the planned economy" (37). On one hand, effects of the Soviet model included a focus on science and technology, limited pedagogical exchange across disciplines, separation of teaching and research, and isolation of Chinese scholars from scholars outside the Soviet sphere. On the other hand, the Soviet model also opened higher education to average Chinese students. Other changes would also dramatically affect Chinese higher education. Through the mid-1960s and 1970s, the Cultural Revolution destroyed many academic freedoms and severely curtailed research in the humanities and social sciences. By the 1990s, China's higher education was again undergoing a massive transformation, this time with expansion of college enrollments from 3.2 million to 18.8

million within a ten-year period (1997-2007). Economic transformation brought on double-digit gains in the gross domestic product (GDP) and a corresponding demand for a better-educated workforce.

Second, WAC origin narratives are important in documenting the cultural and political forces that shape higher education within national contexts, including contexts outside the US, because such narratives offer context for the forces that give rise to WAC initiatives. In doing so, they disrupt notions that WAC is being exported as a complete system from the US and being taken up "as is" in other national contexts. Today, Wu Dan explains, the introduction of WAC into China has the potential to take root because of national awareness that the quality of Chinese higher education must improve. In addition, efforts to expand access to college education as well as provide English language instruction from middle school through college provide a fertile context in which WAC may flourish. Such an opportunity is distinct, however, from other national contexts because it is found in a culture that values Confucianism, includes an appreciation for "good writing" (28), and has adopted an economic growth model that demands highly skilled workers with English language skills. Moreover, it is written against an educational infrastructure that continues to rebuild from the destruction of the Cultural Revolution, limits faculty expansion to match student enrollment increases, and rests on a funding and political model that is resistant to grassroots changes: "in China, grassroots movements could cause unnecessary resistance from the administration who may fear that the initiative or the subsequent research and collaboration may be subversive" (37). Such forces suggest that the uptake of WAC in China will be anything but "as is" from the US.

It would be inaccurate, however, to suggest that the origins of WAC in China and the pressures that Chinese WAC scholars face are entirely unlike the pressures faced by American scholars. One of the things that struck me in reading *Introducing Writing Across the Curriculum into China: Feasibility and Adaptation* was the similarity of challenges that Chinese and American WAC scholars face. Like the US, for example, Chinese higher education values science and technology over degrees in the humanities and social sciences, is driven by an assessment system that—although different than the US accreditation process—drives many of the decisions made by university administrators, and is based on a reward system for faculty that privileges research over teaching.

These differences and similarities become more evident through Wu Dan's twenty-eight interviews with Chinese faculty, administrators, and recruiters in Beijing and Xi'an as well as eight interviews with US-based WAC scholars. Despite the carefulness by which Wu Dan describes her narrative protocol, I found myself wanting more in the methods from this project. In fact, one of my criticisms of this project is that it seems to rely solely on interviews for its explanatory powers.

Qualitative researchers will find this lack of triangulation difficult. Where is the analysis of artifacts, samples of student writing, interviews with students, or survey results? Such methodological triangulation would have allowed Wu Dan to make stronger claims about the importance of her findings and directions for future research.

Notwithstanding my quibbles about the methodological approach in this project, I found myself intrigued by Wu Dan's findings, which are divided into primary and secondary themes depending on the frequency of the topic in the interview data. Not surprisingly, Chinese interview participants universally agreed that strong communication skills were important in the workplace. Moreover, almost all agreed that communication skills should be taught in higher education because communication skills are a "basic competence" (64), allow for the demonstration of technical competence, and are lifelong skills. What's interesting here is that in these interviews there is a view of writing in which writing is not distinct from acquisition of technical content—a point captured by one human resources (HR) manager. Wu Dan summarizes: "Chinese engineers can do as well as their Europeans counterparts, but the European engineers present their work more effectively. The reason, [the HR manager explained], was not the quality of the knowledge or skills of the Chinese engineers, but their lack of communication practice in the universities" (64). There was also a strong belief among participants that student writing both in Chinese and English was not very good (although professional recruiters were less critical of student writing in Chinese). It seems that Chinese and US faculty and business-sector professionals share many of the same attitudes toward student writing, even if they don't share the same cultural context.

What was also intriguing in interviewee responses was that there was no discourse of falling standards or cataclysmic cultural downfall as are standard themes in US popular literacy discourse. Writing did not need to be added to the curriculum. Instead, in interview responses there was a discourse of writing that was intermeshed with education and work. In fact, as Wu Dan concludes, WID is already present in Chinese higher education but "without proper guidance or support" (107). Writing is generally perceived as a by-product of courses, not evidence of student learning. While Wu Dan sees this as a fault, it's useful to note that writing is present in Chinese higher education and that it is perceived as a transparent process of acquiring technical knowledge. Finally, participants' views of writing were deeply tied to the global economy and the desire of interviewees to integrate intercultural communication into the curriculum. One wonders what US WAC would look like today if intercultural communication had been one of its initial theoretical pillars.

Despite this integrated view of writing and the consensus among interviewees that campus-wide communication initiatives might work best, interviews revealed strong disincentives to introducing WAC-based programs, including issues such as heavy faculty workloads, assessment systems that are misaligned with writing outcomes, insufficient technological support, and mercurial administrative support.

Wu Dan's findings from her interviews with the eight American WAC scholars were less enlightening to me, in part, because such perspectives are well known in US scholarship. One exception, however, was her findings related to international dissemination of WAC. Interestingly, interviewees suggested that US WAC scholars have gained quite a bit of expertise in learning about international contexts for WAC. This marks an important change in the field and one worth continuing to follow in the scholarship; WAC of the future might be equally informed by the work outside of the US as well as the work within the US It was particularly heartening that the US interviewees all agreed that the future of WAC is enriched through internationalization of the field.

In conclusion, Wu Dan argues that the results of her research "strongly support" the feasibility of WAC in mainland China (118). She offers the following advice for implementing successful WAC programs in mainland China: 1) administrative independence of writing/study centers from any department or college; 2) secure funding; 3) faculty development and connections with the evaluation program; and 4) faculty rewards such as reduced workload. She also concludes that obstacles in the way of implementing WAC in China include the local higher education structure, academic dishonesty, and insufficient educational technology resources.

Wu Dan writes, "With China now being the home of the most English-language speakers in the world and its rapidly increased access to higher education, the timing has never been more optimal for bridging the Chinese needs [for quality writing instruction] and the US-based WAC initiative" (119). Indeed, the introduction of WAC into China offers the possibility of a powerful new vision for writing instruction across the curriculum. *Introducing Writing Across the Curriculum into China: Feasibility and Adaptation* gives us a portrait of that potential.

PARLOR PRESS
EQUIPMENT FOR LIVING

New Media Theory   **New Releases**   **For WPAs**

EXPLORE INTERACTIVE PRINT!
Download the free Layar App
then scan this page →

The entire Parlor Press catalog will be out in ePub, iPad, iBook, and Kindle formats in late 2013, some with embedded video, audio, and more sensory symbolic action. Watch for innovative integration of social reading platforms (Social Book, Book2Look), distribution/affiliate technologies (ReKiosk), Augmented Reality, and more.

www.parlorpress.com
3015 Brackenberry Drive, Anderson, SC 29621 | 765.409.2649 (p)

Contributors

Jennifer Ahern-Dodson is Director of Outreach for the Thompson Writing Program at Duke University. Her research and teaching interests center on learning communities, new media, civic engagement, and faculty writing, and she has published articles and book chapters on writing-to-learn pedagogies and community-university partnerships. While at Duke she has been involved in a number of interdisciplinary community engagement initiatives focused on public scholarship and developed writing-based partnerships with K-5 schools. She also leads multidisciplinary faculty learning communities that explore pedagogical innovations in writing and undergraduate research. Her current work includes the Faculty Write Program, which focuses on faculty-as-writers and fostering conversations about the intersections between faculty writing, teaching, and research.

Laura Brady is Eberly Professor of Outstanding Teaching within the English department at West Virginia University, where she also directs the composition program. She is currently working with colleagues across campus to initiate a communication-across-curriculum program. Her research often focuses on writing pedagogy and writing program administration and has appeared in *WPA: Journal of the Council of Writing Program Administrators*, *Composition Forum*, *College English*, and several other journals and edited collections.

Denise Comer is an Assistant Professor of the Practice of Writing Studies and Director of First-Year Writing at Duke University. She teaches theme-based first-year writing seminars on such areas of inquiry as illness narratives, civic engagement, and travel writing. Her scholarship, which has been published in such journals as *Pedagogy and Composition Forum*, explores writing pedagogy, writing program administration, and the intersections between technology and the teaching of writing. She has two books forthcoming from Fountainhead Press in 2014: *Writing in Transit: A Reader* (ed.) and *It's Just a Dissertation: The Irreverent Guide to*

Transforming Your Dissertation from Daunting to Doable to Done (co-written with Barbara Gina Garrett). She lives in Raleigh, North Carolina, with her husband and their three children.

Jonathan Hall is Assistant Professor of English at York College, City University of New York, where he is also Writing Across the Curriculum Coordinator and teaches writing and literature courses. His work has appeared in *Across the Disciplines* and will be included in the upcoming books *WAC and Second Language Writers: Research towards Developing Linguistically and Culturally Inclusive Programs and Practices* ed. Michelle Cox and Terry Myers Zawacki and *ReWorking English in Rhetoric and Composition: Language, Locations, Interventions*, ed. Bruce Horner and Karen L. Kopelson. This is his third article for *The WAC Journal*.

Mya Poe is Assistant Professor of English at Penn State University. Her research focuses on writing in the disciplines, writing assessment, and racial identity. Her publications include *Learning to Communicate in Science and Engineering: Case Studies From MIT* (MIT Press, 2010), which won the CCCC 2012 Advancement of Knowledge Award, *Race and Writing Assessment* (Peter Lang, 2012), as well as articles in *CCC* and *JBTC*. Along with Tom Deans, she is editor of the Oxford Short Guides to Writing in the Disciplines. She is currently working on a book entitled *The Consequences of Writing Assessment: Race, Multilingualism, and Fairness*.

Heather M. Robinson is Assistant Professor of English at York College, of the City University of New York, where she also directs the Writing Program and has previously been Writing Center Director and a Writing Across the Curriculum Coordinator. She teaches courses in applied linguistics, and in composition at the first-year and junior level. Her writing has appeared in the *Journal of Basic Writing, TESOL Journal, Writing Lab Newsletter*, and she also has a Program Profile of WAC and Writing at York, written with Michael J. Cripps, forthcoming in *Composition Forum*. She is currently working on a book entitled *The Ethics and Economics of Grammar Instruction*.

David R. Russell, Professor of English, has published widely on writing in the disciplines and professions, international writing instruction, and computer-supported collaborative learning. All are theorized with cultural-historical activity theory and genre theory. His book, *Writing in the Academic Disciplines: A Curricular History*, examines the history of American writing instruction since 1870. He co-edited a special issue of *Mind, Culture, and Activity* on writing research, *Writing Selves/ Writing Societies: Research from Activity Perspectives*, and *Writing and Learning in*

Cross-National Perspective: Transitions from Secondary to Higher Education. He edits *Journal of Business and Technical Communication.*

Carol Rutz directs the writing program at Carleton College, which involves teaching writing and working with WAC faculty on assessment and faculty development. Recent research has involved seeking evidence that faculty development programs affect student learning as well as the teaching practices of individual faculty.

Martha A. (Marty) Townsend is Associate Professor of English at the University of Missouri (MU), where she teaches graduate and undergraduate courses in Composition Studies and where she directed MU's Campus Writing Program from 1991 to 2006. In 2004, she and CWP colleagues Martha Patton and Jo Ann Vogt hosted the 7th National WAC Conference, for which they elected the conference's first-ever international theme; the conference has subsequently become the International WAC Conference. Marty's international workshops and consultations on WAC have taken her to a dozen countries. Most recently, she collaborated with two US colleagues to facilitate Russia's 16th annual Fulbright Foundation Summer School for the Humanities (the first to feature academic writing), hosted by Lomonosov Moscow State University.

Denise Vrchota is an assistant professor in the Communication Studies Program, Department of English at Iowa State University. Her research area is communication in the disciplines. She has published in *Communication Education* and the *Journal of Food Science Education.*

Terry Myers Zawacki is Associate Professor Emerita of English and Director Emerita of Writing Across the Curriculum at George Mason University. She is lead editor on the International Exchanges on the Study of Writing series on the WAC Clearinghouse, co-editor of the forthcoming *WAC and Second Language Writers: Research towards Linguistically and Culturally Inclusive Programs and Practices,* and serves on the CCCC Committee on the Globalization of Postsecondary Writing Instruction and the Scientific Committee of the International Society for the Advancement of Writing Research. She has given invited talks in Europe and the Middle East, in addition to China.

PARLOR PRESS
EQUIPMENT FOR LIVING

New Releases Fall 2013

A Rhetoric for Writing Program Administrators
Edited by Rita Malenczyk. 471 pages.

Thirty-two contributors delineate the major issues and questions in the field of writing program administration and provide readers new to the field with theoretical lenses through which to view major issues and questions.

Writing Program Administration and the Community College
Heather Ostman. 241 pages.

From the history of the community college in the United States to current issues and concerns facing writing programs and their administrators and instructors, *Writing Program Administration and the Community College* offers a comprehensive look into writing programs at the public two-year institutions.

Recently Released . . .

The WPA Outcomes Statement—A Decade Later
Edited by Nicholas N. Behm, Gregory R. Glau, Deborah H. Holdstein, Duane Roen, and Edward M. White.

Writing Program Administration at Small Liberal Arts Colleges
Jill M. Gladstein and Dara Rossman Regaignon.

Rewriting Success in Rhetoric and Composition Careers
Edited by Amy Goodburn, Donna LeCourt, and Carrie Leverenz.

and with the WAC Clearinghouse . . .

Writing Programs Worldwide: Profiles of Academic Writing in Many Places
Edited by Chris Thaiss, Gerd Bräuer, Paula Carlino, Lisa Ganobcsik-Williams, and Aparna Sinha

International Advances in Writing Research: Cultures, Places, Measures
Edited by Charles Bazerman, Chris Dean, Jessica Early, Karen Lunsford, Suzie Null, Paul Rogers, and Amanda Stansell

www.parlorpress.com

How to Subscribe

The WAC Journal is published annually in print by Parlor Press and Clemson University. Digital copies of the journal are simultaneously published at The WAC Clearinghouse in PDF format for free download. Print subscriptions support the ongoing publication of the journal and make it possible to offer digital copies as open access. Subscription rates: One year: $25; Three years: $65; Five years: $95. You can subscribe to The WAC Journal and pay securely by credit card or PayPal at the Parlor Press website: http://www.parlorpress.com/wacjournal. Or you can send your name, email address, and mailing address along with a check (payable to Parlor Press) to Parlor Press, 3015 Brackenberry Drive, Anderson SC 29621. Email: sales@parlorpress.com

Pricing

One year: $25 | Three years: $65 | Five years: $95

Publish in The WAC Journal

The editorial board of The WAC Journal seeks WAC-related articles from across the country. Our national review board welcomes inquiries, proposals, and 3,000 to 6,000 word articles on WAC-related topics, including the following:

- WAC Techniques and Applications
- WAC Program Strategies
- WAC and WID
- WAC and Writing Centers
- Interviews and Reviews

Proposals and articles outside these categories will also be considered. Any discipline-standard documentation style (MLA, APA, etc.) is acceptable, but please follow such guidelines carefully. Submissions are managed initially via Submittable (https://parlorpress.submittable.com/submit) and then via email. For general inquiries, contact Heather Christiansen, the managing editor, via email (wacjournal@parlorpress.com). The WAC Journal is an open-access, blind, peer-viewed journal published annually by Clemson University, Parlor Press, and the WAC Clearinghouse. It is available in print through Parlor Press and online in open-access format at the WAC Clearinghouse.

www.ingramcontent.com/pod-product-compliance
Lightning Source LLC
Chambersburg PA
CBHW030404170426
43202CB00010B/1483